CAMBRIDGE LIBRARY COLLECTION

Books of enduring scholarly value

Egyptology

The large-scale scientific investigation of Egyptian antiquities by Western scholars began as an unintended consequence of Napoleon's invasion of Egypt during which, in 1799, the Rosetta Stone was discovered. The military expedition was accompanied by French scholars, whose reports prompted a wave of enthusiasm that swept across Europe and North America resulting in the Egyptian Revival style in art and architecture. Increasing numbers of tourists visited Egypt, eager to see the marvels being revealed by archaeological excavation. Writers and booksellers responded to this growing interest with publications ranging from technical site reports to tourist guidebooks and from children's histories to theories identifying the pyramids as repositories of esoteric knowledge. This series reissues a wide selection of such books. They reveal the gradual change from the 'tomb-robbing' approach of early excavators to the highly organised and systematic approach of Flinders Petrie, the 'father of Egyptology', and include early accounts of the decipherment of the hieroglyphic script.

Koptos ~ Qurneh

Among the leading Egyptologists of his day, Sir William Matthew Flinders Petrie (1853–1942) excavated over fifty sites and trained a generation of archaeologists. This single-volume reissue brings together two of his well-illustrated excavation reports. The first, originally published in 1896, covers the work undertaken in 1893–4 at Koptos (modern-day Qift), a key settlement in Upper Egypt on the Nile's east bank. This includes a chapter on classical inscriptions by D.G. Hogarth (1862–1927). The second report, first published in 1909, discusses recent archaeological work around Qurna in the Theban necropolis, including the discovery of an intact royal burial dating from the seventeenth dynasty. The epigraphic material is addressed in a chapter by James Herbert Walker (d.1914). Petrie wrote prolifically throughout his long career, and a great many of his other publications – for both specialists and non-specialists – are also reissued in this series.

Cambridge University Press has long been a pioneer in the reissuing of out-of-print titles from its own backlist, producing digital reprints of books that are still sought after by scholars and students but could not be reprinted economically using traditional technology. The Cambridge Library Collection extends this activity to a wider range of books which are still of importance to researchers and professionals, either for the source material they contain, or as landmarks in the history of their academic discipline.

Drawing from the world-renowned collections in the Cambridge University Library and other partner libraries, and guided by the advice of experts in each subject area, Cambridge University Press is using state-of-the-art scanning machines in its own Printing House to capture the content of each book selected for inclusion. The files are processed to give a consistently clear, crisp image, and the books finished to the high quality standard for which the Press is recognised around the world. The latest print-on-demand technology ensures that the books will remain available indefinitely, and that orders for single or multiple copies can quickly be supplied.

The Cambridge Library Collection brings back to life books of enduring scholarly value (including out-of-copyright works originally issued by other publishers) across a wide range of disciplines in the humanities and social sciences and in science and technology.

Koptos

~

Qurneh

W.M. Flinders Petrie

CAMBRIDGE
UNIVERSITY PRESS

University Printing House, Cambridge, CB2 8BS, United Kingdom

Published in the United States of America by Cambridge University Press, New York

Cambridge University Press is part of the University of Cambridge.
It furthers the University's mission by disseminating knowledge in the pursuit of
education, learning and research at the highest international levels of excellence.

www.cambridge.org
Information on this title: www.cambridge.org/9781108066143

© in this compilation Cambridge University Press 2013

This edition first published 1896 and 1909
This digitally printed version 2013

ISBN 978-1-108-06614-3 Paperback

KOPTOS.

BY

W. M. FLINDERS PETRIE, D.C.L., LL.D.,

*MEMBER OF THE IMPERIAL GERMAN ARCHÆOLOGICAL INSTITUTE, AND OF
THE SOCIETY OF NORTHERN ANTIQUARIES.*

WITH A CHAPTER BY

D. G. HOGARTH, M.A.

LONDON:

BERNARD QUARITCH, 15, PICCADILLY, W.

1896.

LONDON:
PRINTED BY WILLIAM CLOWES AND SONS, Limited,
STAMFORD STREET AND CHARING CROSS.

CONTENTS.

LIST OF FORTY-SIX ROYAL NAMES FOUND AT KOPTOS.

LIST OF PLATES.

INTRODUCTION.

1. Among the few places which promised to throw some light on the beginnings of Egyptian civilization, Koptos, about thirty miles north of Thebes, was the most available for exploration; having, therefore, obtained permission of the Egyptian authorities, I arrived there on 3rd December, 1893, accompanied by Mr. Quibell. We worked there till I left on 26th February, leaving Mr. Quibell to finish the packing and removal of objects. The twelve weeks thus spent in excavation sufficed to entirely clear over the temple site, besides doing much miscellaneous work about the town.

Kuft, the modern town, is situated mainly on the north-west of the ancient site; but all round the ruins are small hamlets and settlements. The position is now in the midst of the belt of cultivated land on the eastern side of the Nile, about two miles from the river and the same from the desert. But from the configuration of the base soil, it seems not improbable that the river ran close to the western side of the town in the earliest times. That the Nile was at some distance in Ptolemaic times is shewn by the tale of Setna, where the priests of Koptos come down to the boats; and Setna goes to the haven from Koptos; and the existence of a canal in Roman times—probably, as now, a little west of the town—is shewn by the bridge inscription. Hence the general features of the country there do not seem to have altered in the last two thousand years.

2. We settled at Koptos in the midst of the ruins. The massive crude-brick wall of the square Roman temenos included the temple and part of the town; it was much destroyed, being dug away below for earth by the *sebakhin*, but part of the north side was in fair preservation. In a corner-space formed by one of the great bastions, projecting from the wall, we built our huts, and so secured ourselves from the sun and from the strong winds, under the shelter of the great wall. The *sebakhin* were continually digging about, for the earth of the lower part of the wall and beneath it suited their fancy for the fields. And we lived in peaceful security until one morning a thundering vibration was felt, and we found that half the thickness of our wall had been so undermined on the other side that it slipped away into a loose heap of hundreds of tons of broken bricks. As it left a very narrow and perilous pinnacle on our side just over our huts, we had to move a little out of the way; indeed, it seemed a wonder that a few tons had not fallen over and flattened us entirely.

The Kuftis proved to be the most troublesome people that I have ever worked with. The pertinacity with which the rascals of the place would dog our steps about our house, and at the work, was amazing. And the regularity with which a fresh spy was set on every morning, to try and watch our doings, was most irritating. The question each day between Mr. Quibell and myself was, "Have you seen the spy?" and whichever sighted him first at once described him. The purpose of this spying was to know where anything important was found, in order that the dealers might go and work the part by night. Some slabs of sculpture were taken one night; and another time when we had made a discovery, we thought well to go down about ten o'clock, with a tent, to sleep over the place. We found that a party of men were just coming up, and they continued to lurk around for some time in the dark, their dogs barking at us so long as they were about. It became therefore needful to detect the spy every day as soon as we could, and to drive him off. He could generally be noted by being rather better dressed than the workmen, suitably for lounging and not for hard work. One man tried to foist himself into the middle of the temple, professing to want earth from there. He would not go by words, so we came to a struggle; my workmen helped to touzle him, and he went away furious. A few days

B

later I met him when walking alone in a distant hamlet; he followed me respectfully while I was surveying, and I heard him remark about me to another man: "That is a good man, he is firm." He would probably have been a good friend afterwards, had I needed him. Another spy tried to stroll up and down, and we arrested him and took him to his shekh in the village; that dignitary at once disowned him, and said he was a stranger from Koseyr. So the next spy that came strolling, and talking to passers-by on the road as an excuse, we laid down and beat soundly. Still fresh spies came on, until I stalked one and seized his head-shawl; I told him he could have it returned to his shekh, only he must give me the name of the shekh and of himself before he could get it. That no spy would do, for fear of the police; so by the time I had four little bundles of head-shawls laid by, each duly docketted with description of the owner, the spy plague ceased. I give this trouble and its cure as an object lesson in dealing with Egyptians. The only way to lay hold of a man is to confiscate his goods, and leave him to complain; this he will never do if he knows that he was in the wrong.

On many days, fully half my time was taken up by the spy business. The old guard of the museum was quite powerless, as they were his own neighbours, whom he dared not offend. But he sometimes plucked up courage, and took a head-shawl. He was a very good guard, as Egyptians go; he had been a professional thief in his youth, a profession that is not badly thought of, and has—or used to have—a regular guild and shekh of its own. Having retired he made a watchful and trusty guard, very smart with the *nebut* or single stick; often he would challenge a lad, and with a few playful turns would parry the fellow's stick and give him a ringing little crack on his head. I should say he could have stunned any one in a few seconds; how much practice had made perfect we do not know.

Among this rather untoward people we found however, as in every place, a small percentage of excellent men; some half-dozen were of the very best type of native, faithful, friendly, and laborious, and from among these workmen we have drawn about forty to sixty for our work of two following years at Negadeh and at Thebes. They have formed the backbone of my upper Egyptian staff, and I hope that I may keep these good friends so long as I work anywhere within reach of them. Beside these I had living with me at Koptos four of the Illahunis from the Fayum; and some of the former workers from Tell el Amarna came also, but did not prove satisfactory.

3. As I have already said, Mr. Quibell was working with me the whole time; and the latter half of the time we were joined by Mr. Grenfell, who wished to watch some work while studying the Greek materials which he had obtained elsewhere. Mr. Hogarth, who visited us at Koptos, has kindly undertaken the editing of all the classical inscriptions that we found at the site. We were much helped by the cordial kindness of Shekh Bishara Nakhleh of Qus, who sent us continual supplies. Men of such a type are the best strength of the country; with commanding wealth and position, yet unostentatious and free from oppressiveness, enjoying the confidence of all around. Especially happy is it to see such a type not spoiled by any aping of European ways and fashions, but living a purely native life, and serving as an example of what his countrymen may be on the natural basis of their own civilization. There was also another excellent native landowner, who had a large farm close to us, and who occasionally called on us. It was pleasing to see the affectionate manner of every one towards him, and to hear the high character that he had among the peasantry. So long as such men of position are to be found in the country, there is good hope of a better tone being fostered than now exists among the classes eaten up by corruption and intrigue. The recent policy of enquiring into the characters borne by the principal men in a district, and placing power in the hands of those who shew themselves fit to use it, is undoubtedly the right way to give stability and success to the country.

The excavations during this year have been carried on at the charge of my two friends, Mr. Jesse Haworth and Mr. Martyn Kennard, who have in past years likewise done so much to help in furthering Egyptian studies and clearing up the history of the land. The experiment of enlarging the work by having further supervision through Mr. Quibell, and partly through Mr. Grenfell, who was travelling on the Craven Fellowship, has proved so desirable, that after this season the Egyptian Research Account was started as a student fund. The success of that belongs to the tale of the following years. I have to thank Miss Murray for copying from the paper squeezes most of the inscriptions here published.

4. Some general remarks on the nature of the site may be made here before proceeding to describe the

recent excavations and results. The valley from the Nile to the Red Sea, known as the Hammamat Valley, has always been the key to the East. In prehistoric times the Punite race probably entered the Nile valley by this line, and the Egyptians used to send out eastern expeditions by the same route. When commerce became established with Arabia and India in Greek and Roman times, Koptos became the port of the Oriental trade. In Arab times the same course was followed, only diverted to the south, to the neighbouring town of Qus, and still later to the northern town of Qeneh; and the route is still followed, as by the Indian troops in this century. There has been some question as to whether the Copts of modern Egypt received their name in Arabic from Koptos, or from Aegyptos, which is usually derived from *Ha-ka-ptah*, the name of Memphis. There are other names which may help to explain this: the Phoenicians were known to the Egyptians as Kefti; and in India the inlaid work of patterned metal—which we first know of on Aah-hotep's dagger and axe—is known as Kuft work. An hypothesis which would connect all these names might be framed thus: the Kefti or Phoenician—Punite—race settled on the Nile in prehistoric times, and their town was named Keft from them: the inlaid metal work was known as Kuft work in the East, owing either to its Egyptian or Phoenician origin, and Kuft being the port of Egypt to the East, through which all Arabian trade went, the Egyptian became known as a Kufti to the Arab; so that on the Arabian invasion the name was retained for the whole of the indigenous population of Egypt. In the classical form of the name, Koptos, *p* must have been sounded soft, more as a Spanish *b*; in Egyptian the form is Kebti, the *b* here being equal to our *v*, and sounding therefore as Kevti, and the Arabic form is Kuft. The *k* is the *koph* or *q*, which is sounded at present in Upper Egypt as a hard *g*.

CHAPTER I.

THE RISE OF KOPTOS.

5. The natural features of the country have rendered the site of Koptos of importance in history. The Nile in Middle and Lower Egypt runs down the line of the great fault from south to north; but above that it has a direction at right angles from east to west, determined by a great cross valley which stretches from the Red Sea into the Libyan Desert. This valley must have held a wide sheet of water at the time when the Nile was far fuller than it is now. And in the bottom of this lake a bed of tenacious yellow clay was laid down, from the drainage of the eastern mountains which ran into it. This bed became cut away by the later drainage in many parts, after the elevation of the land, and deeper cutting of the Nile valley; but a mass of it remained high above the Nile deposits, and formed a knoll which projected through the flat expanse of black Nile mud around it. This knoll, of much the appearance of London clay, lay just in the track of the only practicable route from the Nile valley out to the Red Sea; and giving a raised site close to the river, amid the swamps and inundations which covered its banks, the early settlers readily adopted it for their dwelling.

6. When we come to uncover this yellow basal clay beneath the later town of Koptos, we find it dug out into many pits over its surface. These were probably holes from which clay had been taken for wattle and daub huts. And in these pits, and strewing over the surface of the clay, lie many flint implements. One fine knife (PL. II, 6) lay in a pit, and many rectangular flint flakes (PL. II, 17, 24, 25) trimmed with square ends, such as we know to belong to the IIIrd—IVth dynasties at Medum, were found strewing about wherever we reached the base level. No traces of palaeolithic man appeared here, although such are found commonly in the neighbouring desert; and this accords with the country having been far deeper under water during the earlier ages of man. Along the west of the clay island it was found to slope down very steeply, and over the slope was thrown out a bed of at least five feet thick of fine black ashes. From the steepness of the slope, which indicated rapid water-wearing, and the throwing of rubbish which suggested that there was no occupant of the ground below, it seems likely that the river-bed ran then close to the island of clay. There is now a large canal about half a mile to the west, and it is possible that this is the somewhat shifted descendant of an old arm or course of the Nile. The period of this ash-bed is roughly shewn by our finding about 40 inches above the base of it a fine flint knife of the back-curved type (II, 1) and a bangle of gold wire (II, 2) (Univ. Coll.). It belonged therefore to the early metal period, when flint was yet in full use; and such a civilization lasted probably for several centuries next before the historical

age of the IVth dynasty. It seems therefore that though Koptos belongs to the dawn of history, its occupation does not stretch far back into the prehistoric age.

Beside the flint implements there was another class of stone-working which may be rather later in origin. Axes of quartzose rock (II, 7–13) are often found in the lower levels of the town (Univ. Coll.); but we did not happen to discover any well placed in our own working, so that the exact positions cannot be stated. The regions from which they have been gleaned by the village boys are both cleared down to early levels; on the south of the temple, and on the northwest, the natives have dug the earth-ruins away, until further work is difficult from the depth of potsherds and stones left behind. On sinking further in these parts I found that the basal clay is at a lower level than it is beneath the temple, which was founded on the highest point; and it appeared that the axes must belong to the lowest yard or two of the town ruins, but not be of the age of the first settlement. The absence of them from our own work is accounted for by our clearances being in the temple area. That space was occupied by the flint-using settlement, but was later enclosed as sacred before the axe-makers dwelt there. In the IVth dynasty the forecourt of the temple (about the third pylon) was common ground, as we there found habitations, and large quantities of pottery of the regular style of the Medum vases. Yet although many rectangular flints were found, as at Medum, no stone axes appeared. It seems then not unlikely that these stone axes belong to the Old Kingdom down perhaps to the VIth dynasty. The types vary from the plain ovoid to the wide axe with lugs; and as one of the latter in hornstone, and others in flint, were found at Kahun in the XIIth dynasty, there is no reason that they should not extend over the earlier historic age here. That they are so much commoner here than elsewhere is easily accounted for by the nearness of the mountains of primitive rock in the Hammamat Desert.

7. The remains of dwellings in front of the temple show that the compact clay was found to be unpleasant as a soil, and careful arrangements were made to obtain a dry floor. We found dozens of cylindrical pots of rough earthenware, inverted, and near together on the ground in regular rows; while over them was about three inches of Nile mud entirely clear of pottery chips. This appears to have been a dry floor made of inverted jars, with a paving of brick laid over them. The types of the pottery, as we have noticed above, are all familiar at Medum; the coarse hand-made jars (Medum XXXI, 15) with a pointed bottom, abounded, and pieces of many varieties of the fine red-faced pottery bowls (M. XXXI, 2–7); the strange thick cup-shaped pots (M. XXXI, 17), with a rough unformed outside over the lower half, were also found. The whole group was a most satisfactory evidence that the types which had been found at Medum were not merely local, but that the same forms and materials characterise this age in Upper Egypt as in the lower country.

8. Of actually dated remains a few pieces of the Old Kingdom were obtained. I bought from a *sebakh* digger on the low ground south of the temple, a piece of a large alabaster jar bearing the name of Khufu (XXI. 3) (Univ. Coll.). From the style of the cutting, and the seated king determinative, it is probably contemporary; and it most likely came from the royal furnishing of the temple of the IVth dynasty. Of the VIth dynasty a small piece, apparently of the front of a statue-throne, bears the *ka* name of Pepy I (Univ. Coll.); and two limestone slabs show scenes of Pepy II (V, 7, 8). These are cut in the local limestone, which is not of good quality, being much fissured, and containing flint nodules. They indicate that a rebuilding done here by Pepy was left to local resources, and did not draw on the royal quarries of fine limestone. These blocks had been removed from the old part of the sanctuary in Ptolemaic times, and were laid face down to fill up some holes in the basal clay beneath the great sand bed of the Ptolemaic temple. One of them shews Pepy offering to a god which was doubtless Min, as the king is named "Beloved of Min" (at Manchester). The other block bears part of the royal figure with a large cartouche (Pepy Ra-nefer-ka) before it, bordered with the early double rope line. Below the scene is a frieze of *dad* signs alternating with figures, the lower parts of which are like the Isiac girdle tie, while above they have the human Hathor head, with cows' ears and horns, as on a sistrum. They seem as if they might be copies of some primitive Hathor idol, which was modified into the sistrum type in later times. In any case they are the earliest Hathor heads of this type that are yet known (Univ. Coll.).

9. In considering the remains found in the temple itself, of an earlier date than the Middle Kingdom, we must take them as a group and disentangle them, without beginning necessarily with the earliest. The main feature of importance for determining the age

was a limestone pavement, in the old sanctuary. This was formed of blocks from a temple of Antef Nub-kheperu-ra, and must therefore have been laid down by a subsequent king. Lately arguments have been brought forward for placing this king and some other Antefs in the XIIIth dynasty instead of the XIth, as has been hitherto reckoned. Yet as no conclusive evidence of the later date has been given, the following reasons seem to fully support the earlier view. (1) No Antef kings appear in the Turin papyrus in the XIIIth dynasty, which is fairly complete at the earlier part of that age. (2) Several Antefs appear in the Karnak table on the side which contains no other kings later than the XIIth dynasty; although that table is confused in order, yet the division in two halves marks a definite epoch, to which the Antefs would be an exception if they belonged to the XIIIth dynasty. (3) The mixture of Antef and Mentuhotep names is constant in families, and on rock graffiti; but Antef and Sebekhotep are not found usually conjoined, pointing to the name Antef being popular in the XIth, but not in the XIIIth dynasty. (4) In the pavement which was composed of the ruins of the Antef temple not a single block of the XIIth dynasty was included. Had Antef belonged to the XIIIth dynasty, the material of the XIIth would have been lying about for later kings to use up along with it. On the contrary in, and beneath, the pavement of Antef slabs not a single trace of the XIIth dynasty was found, plainly suggesting that no sculptures of that age were lying about when it was laid down, and that it must have been so placed during the reconstruction by the XIIth dynasty. We shall continue therefore to treat Antef Nub-kheperu-ra as of the XIth dynasty; for though the evidence is not yet conclusive, it is far stronger than that for the other view.

The age of the laying down of the pavement, which implies the removal of the Antef temple, is therefore probably of the XIIth dynasty. Beneath that there was a bed of about four feet thickness of dark earth and fragments of pottery. Among this were several fragments of the red polished pottery with black tops, and the red polished with white lines, both of which we found in the following year in the tombs of the foreign invaders, or New Race on the opposite shore, and which belong to the VIIth—IXth dynasties. These shew that the invaders had occupied the eastern side, and placed objects in the temple there.

10. In the earth below this pavement was also found a remarkable class of earthenware figures (Oxford). As hardly anything of the same kind was found elsewhere about the temple or town, we must regard these as having been dedicated in the temple, and therefore, as representing the best products of their time, somewhere before the XIIth dynasty. The material of all appears to be ordinary Nile mud, mixed with straw and poorly baked, the oxidation scarcely penetrating the surface, and leaving the interior soft and black. The few rude pieces have no special preparation of the surface; but the greater part of the pottery is faced over with a coat of haematite, finely polished by hand. It does not shew any burnishing lines, and in that is quite different from the polished facing of the New Race pottery; the material and style of baking also differ from that, and no such figures or subjects are known among the great variety of works of the New Race. The material and work therefore shew this pottery cannot be assigned to those invaders.

The subjects of this pottery are various. The rudest and the finest are fragments of human figures and animals, while some large stands are of intermediate style. The figures of the coarse style are without any fine facing, are very roughly pinched into form with the fingers, and have details marked with scored lines. Such are pieces of a human face, and part of a crocodile. Of finer finish are parts of human figures. In one, the trunk (V, 1) has been made as a cylinder, trimmed somewhat oval on the outside, and with cylindrical arms attached at the sides, but with a clear attempt at modelling the shoulder muscles in a careful manner. It shews, in short, traditional rough manufacture being modified by increasing taste. And the finest work is shewn on an arm, which is admirably modelled and finished, the delicate fluctuation over the muscles being rendered with fine skill and knowledge, but quite unobtrusively. A tail of a crocodile is also of similar fine and detailed modelling; and one fragment (V, 3) bears a human head in relief (reading *dep* in hieroglyphics), with the outline of the square mat *p*, the phonetic complement to the head, below it. This shews that hieroglyphs were in use by the makers of this pottery.

We have noted that this pottery must be earlier than the XIIth dynasty; but one object gives a more definite indication of age. A large oval ring-stand of pottery is decorated with relief figures around the outside. It is about ten inches high, and is worn on the upper edge by the rubbing about of a vessel which stood on it. The figures which it bears (V, 2) are roughly modelled, with a flattish surface and clear edges. They represent two hunting-dogs sniffing the ground, while between them is the old motive of a bunch of two lotus flowers tied together. That lotus group is only found on the earliest IVth dynasty tombs, excepting occasional reappearances copied from them in later times. And the dogs have collars on them made of several turns of rope; such collars and such a breed of dogs are only shewn in the hieroglyphs of the IIIrd dynasty and beginning of the IVth, as on the panels of Hesy. One piece of this relief pottery was found associated with hand-made jars and rough pots similar to those of the early IVth dynasty at Medum (Med. XXXI., 15, 17).

The age therefore indicated for this pottery modelling is at, or before, the beginning of the IVth dynasty; and to this the considerations of place also lead us. The position shews that it is before the XIIth dynasty. The VIIth–IXth is excluded, because there is no connection whatever between this modelling and the works of that age, now so well known. The IVth–VIth dynasty was an age of too much finish and elaboration for any such rude figures to be at all likely to be dedicated in one of the main temples of the country. To the rising art of the IIIrd, or of the XIth dynasty, these therefore lead us; and the motives of the dog and lotus, as well as the association with the earliest dateable styles of pottery, indicate the earlier of these dates.

11. Let us now notice what this implies. We have here several stages of work, from the rudest pinched and scratched puppets, up to modelling as fine as that of the grand works of the IVth dynasty. These cannot all be referred to one time, considering that when made they were each thought worthy of being dedicated in a great temple. We should see in these, then, a series of developing art; and that is already shewn to belong to development of the first great period of the Old Kingdom. We are then led to conclude that the art of modelling arose in clay work, and reached a high point while such coarse material was used, and finished with an elaboration of which it was not worthy. Such a history is exactly concordant with what is seen otherwise; the stone sculpture is quite unknown until the IIIrd dynasty, when it appears somewhat stiff and archaic, but still with full powers of modelling and technical treatment. Its early stages are nowhere to be seen; but when we recognise in the clay modelling the development from rude imitations of forms to highly developed art, we have at once a school before us in which the skill of the stone sculptor may have been formed.

Can we, then, see surviving in the conventions of the stone sculpture, any traces of the conventions of clay work? The three most striking peculiarities of the stonework, which were so engrained in the Egyptian mind that they lasted down to the latest times, were (1), the left leg advanced; (2), the legs united by a connecting slab; (3), the back pier up the figure. None of these are needful in stonework, but they all have a meaning when modelling in soft mud. (1) The advanced leg gives increased depth from back to front at the weakest part, where it is liable to bend over. (2) The cross connection between the legs increases the sectional area where it is weakest and most liable to yield to the weight of the mass above. (3) The back pier does the same, and stiffens the whole figure; in clay, such a feature was probably due to adding a cluster of reeds plastered over at the back, to stiffen the mass until it was baked. Therefore, we see how every convention of the stonework is fully accounted for by earlier modelling in clay.

When such transference from clay to stone took place would be determined by the acquisition of fresh means of work. To carve the stone freely would need metal tools, as flint would break too readily by blows. And hence the introduction of metal in ordinary use, and the cutting of stone, would probably be the step which would determine the transference of the artist's working from clay to stone. The date when this took place we may glean from the use of stone tools being still very familiar in the Old Kingdom, shewing that metal had not then supplanted them. And a trace of the actual change is preserved when Manetho states that Tosorthros about the middle of the IIIrd dynasty "built a house of hewn stone." Stone cutting was then a novelty, and coeval with that we should expect to find the rise of stone carving. Such a date would agree well to the earliest examples of statuary, and would not be inconsistent with the pottery modelling shewing types that also belong to the beginning of the IVth dynasty.

The general result, then, to which we are led, is that during some considerable period before the IIIrd dynasty art was developing in pottery modelling, from the rudest imitations of men and animals, gradually modified by copying of the muscles and rounding the forms, until it had reached a high pitch of observation and finish. That on the beginning of the common use of metal, the mastery of hewing stone was obtained, and stone became the best material for statuary in such conditions. The skill and taste which had been developed on pottery was transferred to stone at once, so that in probably a single generation highly-finished stone statuary would become usual, without leaving any intermediate stages of abortive attempts and clumsy endeavours. And this beginning of stone carving may be placed about the middle of the IIIrd dynasty, the conventions requisite in clay modelling clinging, however, to the style in stone, and being retained to subsequent ages. Thus we reach a solution of what has hitherto been one of the greatest mysteries in the course of art— how such a finished and detailed style, and such a grand taste, could arise without leaving a long series of endeavours, as in all other countries. The endeavours were in pottery, which has all perished, or been disregarded hitherto. The stone begins when the art was already developed.

12. Turning now to another subject, we find an entirely different style or styles of stone-carving, quite apart from anything known in Egyptian work. The forming of these figures is entirely done by hammer-work, without any trace of chiselling or of metal tools. And in style they stand outside of any line of development to or from the Egyptian statuary. Two classes of these figures are known at Koptos— a class of animals, comprising a bird (V, 6) and three lions (V, 5) (Oxford), and a class comprising parts of three colossi of the local god Min. The first class of these figures, the animals, are of the same nature, and of the same treatment, as the animal figures of the New Race of invaders of the VIIth–IXth dynasties. The positions in which they are found also agree with this. The bird lay in the earth under the pavement of the XIIth dynasty; two of the lions lay on the basal clay in front of the early temple, several feet under the ground and building of the Ptolemaic time which covered them. These may therefore be set down as religious sculptures of the New Race, which go together with the characteristic pottery of the same people found at the same level.

13. But it is a different case with the figures of Min (at Ghizeh Museum and Oxford). The style of these differs much from the New Race sculptures. It is far better and more anatomical, and the animals figured on them in surface-reliefs are more correct and spirited than any carvings known of the New Race. The positions in which these figures were found unfortunately shew nothing, except that they are earlier than the Ptolemaic times, as they lay beneath the thick sand bed of the Ptolemaic temple. How much earlier we cannot prove, but only infer.

The rudest of the three figures is broken off at the knees and the chest, only the legs and waist remaining. This fragment is 69 inches long, and implies a statue 13 feet high, which would weigh nearly two tons. The type is the same in all of these figures. The legs are parallel and joined together, with merely a groove down between them, on front and back. The knees are very roughly indicated. The arms are rudely formed, about half projecting from the surface of the figure. The left hand is in the usual attitude of Min; the right hand is not raised with a whip, as in the figures of historic times, but hangs down the side; the fingers are clenched, and a hole is drilled through the hand, as if for hanging something to it. Down the right thigh hangs a flap of some material in low relief; this is seen to depend from the girdle. There is no other clothing or dress indicated, and this flap may represent a pouch or bag, especially as it bears figures on it, which may imitate embroidery. On the rudest statue (III, 1 ; IV, 1) these figures are : a stag's head, mouth down, with four tines on each horn, and from the mouth a long projection, which appears as if it were a stake, on which the head is spitted through the mouth; below the stag's head are two *pteroceras* shells, upright, each with mouth to the right. The work is remarkably natural, and as artistic and exact as could be expected, working in such a rough manner. The whole of the figure is hammer-dressed; and the objects upon the flap are indicated by hammering the outline as a slight hollow around the figures.

The next of the three figures remains from the arm-pits to the knees. This portion is rather longer than the first one, being 77 inches long, but the original height was about the same, 13 feet. The attitude is precisely the same. The girdle is clearly shewn here, and consists of eight turns of material around the stomach. A girdle similarly composed of a large number of strips of leather, is now worn by the men in this region, not only by the desert-dwellers, the Ababdeh, but also generally among the fellahin. The knees are better indicated, and the whole shews more desire for finish. But the surface-sculptures on the flap (III, 2 ; IV, 2) are less precisely natural and explicit, more conventional, and just what might be expected as a later development. The subjects are—two tall poles with a similar emblem on the top of each, two saws of saw-fish of the Red Sea, and two *pteroceras* shells below. The emblem on the pole is manifestly an archaic form of the regular hieroglyph for the god Min, with the addition of a feather on the top. This form with the feather is only known on Egyptian work in one case, a coffin of the VIth dynasty in the Ghizeh Museum. The feather also occurs above a Min sign, which is set on the top of a tall pole (rather more conventional than this, and nearer to the hieroglyphic form), carved on one of the mysterious slate slabs with archaic figures and hieroglyphs found at Abydos (see Louvre).

The third and apparently latest figure is broken at the ancles and fork, only leaving the legs, which are 66 inches long. The work is more finished, the line dividing the legs is deeper, the knee-marking is more elaborated, and there is a fine tense curve in the thighs, though no anatomical distinctions of muscles are shewn. The attitude and arrangement appear to have been like the other statues. The surface-carvings, however, are more numerous; but they are less carefully natural, and more conventional (III, 3; IV, 3). In place of the saw of the saw-fish being scrupulously hammered in outline, it is merely scored with incised lines cut by a flint. The whole group consists of the two poles, with Min emblems and feathers; an additional pole with knobs on it between them; the two saws of saw-fish; an ostrich below one pole; the two *pteroceras* shells, mouths to right; the forepart of an elephant, with its feet resting on conical hills; a flying bird (?); and below all, a hyaena chasing a young bull, the feet of both being on conical mounds. The style of the animals is spirited, and shews a good idea of form and expression, though disproportionate and archaic. Beside these, the head of the last one was found (V, 10). It is a rounded lump, without any face, the front being flattened, apparently to have a carved face attached—perhaps of wood. Down the sides is shewn the ribbing for whiskers, but no other hair is indicated; the ears are large and prominent.

14. The question now arises as to the date and origin of these figures of the great god of that region. Of parallels to the type of the Min emblem we have already noted two, one of the VIth dynasty, the other on the slates of unknown age. These slates with relief figures shew many traces of being of prehistoric times, especially the very pictorial and unconventional hieroglyphs, on a piece from Abydos at the Ghizeh Museum. Another instance of this Min sign occurs, on a pole exactly similar with feather and side pendants, as the ensign of galleys on painted pottery from Nagada. This pottery is found in graves of the New Race, who are now believed to be Libyans. But this ware, as well as some other varieties, appears to have been imported and not made by the invaders. The whole case will be seen argued in the description of it; suffice to say here, that the conclusion is that it was probably made on the Mediterranean coast of North Africa, by a people with whom the Libyans traded, but certainly not by the Libyan invaders of Egypt themselves. Thus, of the three instances of such an arrangement of the Min emblem, one is of the VIth, one of the VIIth–VIIIth dynasties, and one apparently before the IVth dynasty. As in all later Egyptian representation the Min hieroglyph became more and more formal, and farther from any resemblance to its earlier type, it does not seem likely that any sudden reversion to an unconventional óriginal would be likely to arise after that was apparently quite forgotten. The mode of working also shews an ignorance of metal tools, and a dependence upon hammering and bruising the stone, which would be very unlikely to be the case after metals were in familiar use in that part of the world. There is, then, a presumption for a prehistoric date for these sculptures.

It may be needful to clear away any supposition that these figures belong to the New Race, whose rude hammer-dressed animal carvings were also found in the temple. The style and subjects of the work preclude our supposing any such connection. No figure of Min is found in all the New Race remains; nor is there among those any instance of the *pteroceras* shell, the saw-fish, the hyaena, or the ox with crescent horns. On the other hand, among the several objects on the Min figures there are none of the sacred animals of the New Race, the couchant lion, the hawk, the dog, or the goat. The styles of work are also very different. The best of the New Race figures has none of the spirit and fidelity shewn in the Min carvings; and in no instance are the feet of animals figured as upon hillocks. While on the Min figures there is no trace of the cross-line hatching which was regularly used by the New Race to cover the bodies of animals. In short both in subjects and in style there is no resemblance between the New Race carvings and the Min statues.

15. Whence, then, came the workers of the Min statues? The objects shewn are all African. The elephant and the ostrich are common to North Africa; for the former, compare the Carthaginian elephants

of Hannibal. But the saw-fish and the *pteroceras* shell imply a people from the sea; and that the Red Sea, rather than the Mediterranean. And, moreover, there is no trace of anything characteristic of the Nile; no crocodile or lotus, as on the primitive pottery, no hippopotamus, no hawk. We are led then to look to the Red Sea, and to suppose that the people from thence had formed their religious ideas and emblems before they entered Egypt. That they resided a long time at Koptos is shewn by the three Min statues varying in style of art and details. Such differences of work in a very early stage imply a considerable difference in time. And the presence of three such colossi, so large that any one would be a notable centre for worship, makes it unlikely that all were used at once; they rather seem to have been each substituted in succession, as the earlier ones became injured.

We are led then to suppose that the statues were wrought by a people ignorant of metals; who resided for several generations at Koptos; who came from the Red Sea as strangers to the Nile, but who had the same worship as the people of Koptos, without borrowing from the Nile; whose Min emblem was in a more primitive and pictorial form than any known in Egyptian carvings, though like some of the earliest examples; and who had real artistic taste and feeling which was steadily developing. These characteristics will, so far as we can at present imagine, only agree in one race, that supposed people from Punt, whom by portraiture and other considerations I have already stated to be probably the founders of the dynastic Egyptian race, the last immigrants who came in before the historic period. If so, a considerable time must have passed for them to adopt Egyptian emblems, as the crocodile, lotus, and hunting dog, upon the primitive pottery; and for the further development of modelling, up to the highest pottery level, which is equal to the fine archaic stone carving of the IIIrd and IVth dynasty. If we suppose some centuries to have elapsed between the earliest Min statue and the finest pottery modelling, it would not be improbable.

16. The nature of the Min emblem we have not yet noted, as it does not bear directly on the age. In historic times we find it a ball between two wedges, in earlier times it was more like a bolt with two rings or shanks on either side of a central ball, on the slate carving it is thicker in proportion, on the boat and ostrich pottery—which is probably Mediterranean—it is like the form on the Min figures, though roughly painted. As it is represented as being on the top of

a tall pole, it cannot be a heavy object; and the form is most like the early mode of shewing a garland upon statues. It seems then most likely that it was a garland of flowers and a feather, on the top of a tall pole, round which hung saws of saw-fish and *pteroceras* shells: in fact, much such a derwish pole as the southern tribes carry about at the present day. The questions of how the same emblem comes to be connected with a people from the Red Sea, and again with a sea-going people in the Mediterranean (on the pottery), we shall discuss when dealing with the New Race in the volume on Naqada.

CHAPTER II.

THE MIDDLE KINGDOM.

17. The earlier remains of this period, as we have already mentioned, are the sculptures of the temple of Antef V (now at Ghizeh, Oxford, Univ. Coll., etc.). From the thinness of the slabs, which are only about three or four inches through, and the absence of any massive blocks of this king's work, it is evident that the bulk of construction was of mud brick, and the sculptures merely faced over the rougher material. These slabs—as we have mentioned—were all found lying face down, forming a rough pavement, over about four feet of earth with chips of early remains. This pavement is shewn on the plan. The Usertesen jamb has fallen northward, and was the southern jamb of the door; the "box" of sandstone probably having contained foundation deposits in the middle of the doorway. The lower block of the jamb is gone, and thus when complete its base would have been south of the box. Hence the Antef pavement occupied the sanctuary of the XIIth dynasty temple. Probably the ground was looked on as too sacred to be disturbed there, and so was reverently covered over with the slabs of the dismantled older temple of the XIth dynasty, above which was probably placed a fine-stone paving for the temple of Amenemhat and Usertesen.

Some of the Antef slabs are in relief, as shewn on PL. VI, 1–6; and the work of these is finer and more detailed than that of the incised blocks 7–18. Several of the portions of scenes here shewn are reconstructed from many separate slabs; No. 16, for instance, is formed of nine pieces, which were found scattered apart.

c

The subjects are of interest as shewing the permanence of many details which we know in later times. The three trees growing up from an irrigated plot behind the statue of Min (VI, 6), and the two serpents in shrines seen in Ptolemaic sculpture are here (VI, 6). The globe and wings of Hor-behudet with the uraei (VII, 13, 14) appear as in later times; and this is the first large example known, the earlier ones of Khufu and Unas being on a smaller scale. The *khaker* ornament was used along the tops of the scenes (VI, 1, 2, 10) as at Beni Hasan. The scenes appear to have been of the same character as those of older times (see Snefru and Khufu, L. D. ii 2; and Pepy, L. D. ii 115, 116). The king smites his enemies before Min (VI, 2), worships Min (VI, 12), and is embraced by the gods (VII, 16). There have been some scenes with goddesses, of which only two slabs remain (VI, 8, 11), unfortunately without names. Of course it is now obvious what the source was of the block of Antef V, built into a bridge at Koptos, and seen by Harris (My. E. 447).

18. Of the same age, though recopied, is a long decree of Antef V, deposing one prince of Koptos, and instating a new princely family. This was engraved on the south side of the east entrance to the temple: so that when the south jamb of the doorway was overthrown northward, its inner side lay beneath, and we discovered the inscription by looking on the underside of the block (PL. VIII). It is now, with the adjacent sculptures, placed in the Ghizeh Museum. As the doorway was built by Usertesen I, there would be a *prima facie* case for an added inscription such as this being later in origin. But against this fact we have to set the improbability of a king in a much poorer age, just after the XIIth dynasty, caring to make additions of baser quality (such as these Antef sculptures) to a magnificent work of the XII dynasty: and the fact that no trace of sculptures from the XIIth dynasty temple was mixed with the Antef blocks when they were laid down to make a pavement. It seems more likely, then, that the inscription was carved on the doorway of the new temple, as being the title-deed of the reigning prince; having been conferred about a century before then, it would be still of practical importance, and might have been called in question by some descendant of the deposed family.

The translation of this inscription is as follows:—

(1) "The third year, month Phamenoth, 25th day, of his majesty the king (Ra·nubu·kheper, sa·ra·, Antef) giving life like the sun for ever. Decree of the king to the chancellor, prince of Koptos, (2) Min·em·hat, the king's son, administrator of Koptos Qa·nen, the chancellor Menkh·Min, the scribe of the temple Nefer·hotep·ur, all the garrison of Koptos, and all the officials of the temple,—

"Behold ye this decree has been (3) brought to you that ye may know that my majesty has sent the scribe and divine chancellor of Amen Amen·se, and the *semsu hayt* Amen·user, (4) to make inquisition in the temple of Min:—

"Whereas the officials of the temple of my father Min came to my majesty to say that an evil thing is come to pass in this (5) temple, even a harbouring of enemies by (blasted be his name) Teta, son of Minhetep:—

"Therefore let him be cast out upon the ground from the temple of my father Min, let him be driven (6) from his office of the temple, to the son of his son, and the heir of his heir; may they be cast abroad upon the earth, let his bread and his sacred meat be seized, let his name not be remembered in this temple, (7) as is done to one like him who has transgressed in the matter of an enemy of his god; let his writings in the temple of Min be destroyed, and in the government office on every roll likewise:—

"And every king (8) and every puissant ruler who shall forgive him, may he not receive the white crown, or support the red crown, or sit upon the throne of Horus the living; let not the two diadems (9) grant him favours as beloved of him; and every administrator or prince who shall approach the Lord to forgive him, let his people, his possessions, and his lands be given to the endowment of (10) my father Min of Koptos; also let not any man of his circle, of the relations of his father or of his mother be raised to this office:—

(11) "Also that this office shall be given to the chancellor, overseer in the palace, Min·em·hat, and let there be given to him its bread and its sacred meat, established unto him in writings in the temple (12) of my father Min of Koptos, to the son of his son and the heir of his heir."

Mr. Griffith, in translating this, remarks that it closely follows the spelling of the hieratic: the repetition of the feminine *t* before suffixes is especially noticeable; and there are a few positive mistakes of spelling. The *qenbet* (ll. 2 and 4) are written as if *unut;* and *zerf,* " written title," is muddled, especially in l. 11, where it was first spelled *zedf.*

Probably also of the XIth dynasty or earlier is a head and part of the base of a statuette, which was found in the earth under the pavement of Antef blocks (Univ. Coll.). It is carved in hard yellow limestone, about a third of life-size. The head is shewn in PL. V, 9 ; it is of careful and expressive work. As the left ear is less prominent and much less finished than the right, it is probable that this is part of a group of two figures seated side by side. The fragment of a base which was found bears the old entwined lotus around the *sam,* and evidently belongs to the head, being of precisely similar stone.

19. The remains of the XIIth dynasty are of far finer work than the foregoing sculptures of Antef V. They begin with Amenemhat I, of whom there is the upper part of a scene (IX, 1) of the king adoring Min. This is carved in very hard limestone, which has been hammer-dressed and then scraped down, as it was probably too hard for the copper chisels then used. The work is superb for design and finish. The most renowned sculptures of later times—those of Sety I, at Abydos—are coarse and mechanical by the side of this work of Amenemhat. The head of Min is repeated on a larger scale here (V, 10) to shew the art : and the exact resemblance between the king and his *ka* behind him should be noticed. The three blocks composing this scene were found face down in the foundations of Tahutmes III, at the east end of the temple. (Univ. Coll.)

Another slab, which from the fineness of the work may be attributed to the same date, is the Nile figure with offerings (XI, 2), in low relief. (Univ. Coll.)

Immediately after this work, and doubtless in the course of the same building of the temple, there were sculptures of Usertesen I erected here. These are not so beautiful in execution as the relief of Amenemhat, but are yet far above any later sculpture known. The style is exactly that of the reliefs on the sides of the seated statues of Usertesen from Lisht. One jamb of the eastern doorway of the temple was found, bearing on its inner face the fine reliefs shewn in PL. X, 2, representing Usertesen offering to Bast and to Nekheb, probably the earliest figures of these goddesses that are known. The two limestone blocks bearing this sculpture are in the Ghizeh Museum.

On the outer face of the jamb was a line of incised inscription (X, 3), which formed a border around the doorway. Another door—of red granite—also stood here (X, 1) ; as the jamb lay to the S.E. of the

limestone jamb (see Plan, PL. I), it probably belonged to an outer gateway. (Oxford.)

Of the internal work of Usertesen one fine scene was found (IX, 2) turned face down at the bottom of the foundations of the Ptolemaic work (see Plan, " Usertesen slab "). It had been covered with a thin film of stucco to receive the paint, and this had perfectly preserved the texture of the stone, so that the surface of the original sculpture was never exposed from the time of Usertesen until I cleaned it in London. The work is very brilliant, though not so delicate as that of the previous reign. The subject of the king dancing, with the oar and *hap,* is known from the VIth dynasty (L. D. ii 116) down to Roman times, in connection with the *sed* festival, as here. (Univ. Coll.)

Another slab, probably of Usertesen I, with the upper part of Min (XI, 3), bears the original colouring in good condition ; the face of Min is black, (now at Manchester). A fragment of a goddess in relief is either of this or the previous reign (X, 4).

20. At the east end of the temple, close to the overthrown south jamb of the door, stood a sandstone box. It was on the basal clay, but disturbed, being turned up on end, with the sunk lid still in place, but the upper end broken open. From its position it had evidently been in the axis of the doorway, where foundation deposits are generally found. Both inside and out it shews the chisel-marks on every side, so that it was never intended to be seen. Hence it seems pretty certain that it was buried, and in the centre of the doorway ; so that it probably contained the foundation deposit, which was to be expected in that position. The end was broken off, and the inside full of earth. I emptied the whole of it most carefully with my own hands, but no traces of the original contents remained. The size of the box is as follows : Outside, $24 \cdot 3 + x$ long, probably 28 inches originally ; $16 \cdot 5$ wide at top, $17 \cdot 9$ below ; $16 \cdot 5$ high. Inside 22 long + perhaps only a few tenths of an inch , $10 \cdot 3$ wide at top, $11 \cdot 4$ at base ; $14 \cdot 0$ deep, less a ledge $2 \cdot 2$ to $2 \cdot 4$ deep. The lid, $12 \cdot 1$ wide ; $1 \cdot 9$ thick. (Univ. Coll.)

In the temple of Illahun the deposits were placed in a square pit in the rock, covered with a block of stone ; and if such were the custom of the XIIth dynasty, it would be likely that they would substitute a stone box with a lid when building on a clay ground, where no such rock-pit could be cut.

21. Of Amenemhat III a colossal vulture was found, lying in a hole in the basal clay. It bore on the upper surface of the pedestal a long cartouche containing

the whole title with the name (XI, 1). "Live Horus, great of spirits, king of Upper and Lower Egypt [Ne-maat-ra], beloved of Sekhemt, mistress of Ankhtaui." This goddess was the consort of Ptah of Memphis, and mother of Imhotep; and it is singular that the maternal emblem, the vulture, should have been dedicated to this fierce goddess, so well known in the lion-headed form. It is one of the earliest sculptures of divine animals that we know. (Ghizeh Museum.)

A few undated fragments of the middle kingdom are also published here. A piece of a funeral stele (XI, 4) shews offerings of three kinds of deer. Another piece of a stele is engraved on both sides (XI, 5, 6), and shews the truly XIth dynasty taste for dogs; on No. 5 the dog is named Hemu-ma, and on No. 6 there is a turn-spit. The inscription is part of a formula known at El Bersheh, naming the deceased as "a boon companion, loving frankincense, partaker of a happy time." This was found laid down in the pavement with the Antef blocks. (Univ. Coll.) Another slab, apparently from some tomb, has a sketch-outline of a boating procession : a dog is again shewn here, apparently named *dep-nefer*. (Univ. Coll.) These are probably all before the XIIth dynasty.

After the XIIth dynasty there is a piece of a basalt stele (XII. 1) referring to officials of the temple and naming the month Epiphi. Also a piece of a lime-stone stele (XII. 2) with the following inscription, for a man who was son of Amena and a royal wife Ha-ankhs, and his wife, "(1) the joy of her husband . . . (2) satisfying the heart of her consort, the king's daughter Sebekemheb (3) (born of?) the principal (royal wife?) Nubemhat. He says, Oh ye who live upon earth, scribes (4) (lectors etc.) . . . priests of the house of Nub who enter into (this) temple, (5) (and worship this image?) of Hathor which I have placed at the staircase of the mistress of . . . (6) (as ye praise your goddess and follow her processional) bark that raises her beauties aloft; and as ye love to see the beauties of Hor-sma-taui (7) (and desire that your children may sit) upon your seats and that ye may pass on your offices to your sons, so (8) (say ye, a royal oblation to Nub ?) in Dendera, Ra Har (akhti ?) and the gods in the upper (mansions) (9) . . . may they give thousands of all things) good and pure (on which) a god lies, and pure bread of the House of Nub (10) (to the ka of . . .) son of the *uartu* of the royal table Amena, born of the royal wife Ha-ankhs." In trans-lating this Mr. Griffith remarks that the goddess *Nub* (l. 4) is a form of Hathor at Dendera from which the temple was named the House of Nub. Hor-sma-taui (l. 6) was the son of the Hathor of Dendera. The "upper mansions" (l. 8) are connected with the solar worship especially at Heliopolis. The reference to this stele in History i. 218, should be corrected, for this does not relate to Sebekhotep IV as Hor-sma-taui, though it is closely of that period.

22. Deep down under the sand-bed of the Ptolemaic temple, in a hole in the basal clay were found the pieces of a stele of king Rahotep. It is carved on a local limestone, like that of Pepy, with many flint nodules. The whole of the scene at the top is lost, excepting just some feet; but the full breadth and height of the inscription remains, though with many gaps. The scene represents Rahotep, with a son behind him, offering to Min. The inscription reads :

"(1) [Year . . . under the] Majesty of Horus pro-longing life, wearer of the two diadems rich in years, hawk of gold flourishing . . . [king of Upper and Lower Egypt Sekhem-uah-khau-ra, son of the] Sun Rahotep giving life (2) . . . [proclamation was made by] his majesty to his nobles, the courtiers who were with him . . . in the temple . . . ' . . . my majesty has found my father (3) [Min, who is at the] head of all the gods ; and his gates and his doors have gone to decay.' They did obeisance before his majesty and said, 'Let thy *ka* command that (4) they be done oh ! king, our lord. Hu (god of taste) is he who dwells in thy mouth, and Sa (god of intellect) is he who [dwells in thy heart]. Ptah Sokar [begat thee and] (5) the gods fashioned thee ; thou workest for them to provide their temples . . . (6) thou hast united the south and the north ; thy heart is enlarged upon the Horus-throne of the living . . . thou rulest the circuit of the sun . . . (7) good . . . of the en-lightened, an asylum for all people ; thou sleepest not at night nor resteth in the day in serving (8) the gods and seeking the good of this land. Ra makes thee as his image to bring forth what is . . . (9) . . . as it was in the time of thy forefathers, the kings who followed Horus.' Never were things destroyed in my days (10) . . . of the things that existed aforetime. I made monuments for the gods. . . ." The remainder is too fragmentary to translate. (XII. 3, Univ. Coll.)

Rahotep appears from this to have been a pious king, preserving and repairing where he could not afford to build. The monuments of this king are so rare that we may notice a stele (yet unpublished) in the British Museum. It is about 18 inches high and 17 wide. The globe, wings, and uraei, in the tym-panum. Below, two lines containing the name of

Rahotep beloved of Asar-Khentamenti of Abydos. Below, a scene of three men offering to Osiris. Below, two lines of an adoration to Osiris by Ptahseankh, etc. At one side of the tablet a man, overseer of the temple ; at the other side a woman, with the title citizeness, *ankht en nut*. It is of very rough work and in bad condition. Some other inscription must have been known to Lepsius, as he gives the throne-name in the Königsbuch. The stele from Koptos however gives, for the first time, the Hor name, the double diadem name, and the Hor-nub name.

Some columns found displaced in the Ptolemaic rearrangement, are probably of the Middle Kingdom. Columns and circular bases are both cut in dark brown sandstone ; the octagonal columns are 14·2 inches across, one circular base is 24 inches across, and another circular base is 41 inches across, and 5½ inches high.

CHAPTER III.

THE NEW KINGDOM.

23. We now turn to the rebuilding of the temple by Tahutmes III (see plan, PL. I). Nothing is known about the surroundings of the temple before Ptolemaic times ; so our present view is restricted to the block of foundations next around the words "Temple of Tahutmes." These foundations are all of sandstone. On the west front are massive piles of blocks about eight feet high, rough in outline, and evidently hidden originally. These are doubtless the foundations of columns or pillars. On the north side is some continuous wall base. And on the south-east a fragment of similar foundations remains, which is of the same age, not only by its work but by the deposit placed with it.

The foundation deposits serve to mark out this building. They are here marked F. D., and numbered 1 to 7. All of these deposits (not those in the two north corners of the outer building) are alike in material, and nearly all bear the name of Tahutmes III. They were early in his reign, as a scarab of Hatshepsut occurred in No. 3. One deposit (5) is in the axis under the entrance on the west. Four separate deposits form a group in the axis at the east end ; and as the door jamb of the XIIth dynasty shews that in that time an eastern door existed, the plan was probably alike under the XVIIIth dynasty. In the middle of the south side another deposit (6) was found ; and from the analogy of deposits of the next dynasty at Thebes, this probably shews where a cross wall divided the temple. And the last deposit (7) was under the south-east corner. No trace of other deposits could be found in parallel positions.

The area of the temple thus indicated is about twice as wide, and rather longer than, the temple of Tahutmes III at Medinet Habu ; and almost the size of the sanctuary-end of the temple of Amenhotep III at Luxor, beyond the open courts. The spacing of the foundations at the west front seems rather extreme for columns, about 16 feet centre to centre ; but such span is used in the XVIIIth dynasty at Luxor, though it is a little more than the spans in the court there. The position suggested for a cross wall by desposit 6, would show that the shrine was not in the centre ; and from plans of other temples of this age it was probably in the front half, and chambers in the back half. Of course it must be remembered that all temples of this age were processional in theory, being resting-places for the sacred bark, with a clear way in and out at both ends ; and hence from the group of deposits at the east end, it is probable that there was an external door there. The well by these deposits goes down below the present water-level ; and though I made great efforts to reach the bottom, the water rose too fast to bale it out. It probably has no connection with the temple, but is one of the old wells of the primitive settlement before any temple was built, as we found several other such wells in the area.

The external appearance of the temple was probably much like that of Tahutmes at Medinet Habu. In the ruins of the Coptic Church, west of the temple, are four standing pillars, and one fallen, which have certainly come from this temple, as they bear scenes of Tahutmes III. They are of red granite, plain below and figured above, exactly like the sculptures of the pillars of Tahutmes at Medinet Habu. They vary somewhat in size, some being 32 × 34 inches, others 32 × 37 inches. We may then figure to ourselves a portico of square red granite pillars along the front, and a building of sandstone behind, containing a shrine for the sacred bark, and a group of chambers for the temple property behind that, divided by the central passage which opened out at the back of the temple, eastward.

24. Turning now to the foundation deposits. These were all placed in circular pits cut in the basal clay. Plans are here given (PL. XVI) of Nos. 1, 2, 3 and 7. Beside these, No. 4 was only a shallow hole without

any regular deposit. On the top of it was a small shell and a flat piece of steatite; in it were a spire shell, and a broken end of a black stone axe, which was almost certainly far older. No. 5 contained only pottery, and was broken up and scattered by the diggers, as I was not at all expecting anything there at the time. No. 6 contained a quantity of copper models of tools and pottery, but was so far cleared by the boys working it before I saw it, that it is not worth drawing here. Had the plan of the temple been perceptible while we were at work, of course such points would have been watched; but the scattered foundations under 8 or 10 feet of earth could not be understood until the work was done; and the definition of the temple was mainly traced out by the position of these deposits. The numbers attached to them shew the order of finding; and it is well that only two out of seven were disturbed by accident, all the other holes being completely recorded by myself.

Deposit No. 1 (PL. XVI). This consisted of five jars (XIV, 40, etc.), an axe (XV, 68), an adze (64), narrow chisel (65), and knife of copper (73), inscribed; and a model corn-grinder stone (XIV, 3), inscribed in ink. These objects lay irregularly in the axis of the temple.

Deposit No. 2 was almost entirely of pottery, the forms of which are shewn in the plan (PL. XVI). On the west side lay an oval piece of alabaster with inscription (XIV, 2); and under the central pot lay some bones.

Deposit No. 3 was the most elaborate by far; the hole was about 25 inches deep. The objects were scattered throughout the whole depth; the deepest are marked with the depth in inches placed *inside* the outlines, while all the reference numbers to PL. XIV, XV, are outside the outlines. At the top of all lay the strange quintuple jar (XIV, 7), formed in smooth, pale, reddish-buff pottery, painted with red and black lines. The two front jars have arms, with hands holding breasts, and apparently two feet turned up in front. A cow has lain across these feet on each jar. Between the front jars is a Hathor cow, with disc and uraeus between the horns; another such cow stands further back; and four scorpions in relief on a flat ground lie between the jars at the sides. The fifth or last jar has lost its neck, and hence does not shew at the top. This group lay in the earth above the hole of the deposit, and was the first object found there. It was a little broken, as there was nothing to give warning of its neighbour-

hood, and it was found just in finishing work at dusk one night. I searched the place that evening, and had to heap loose earth on it to prevent any natives trying it by night. Next day we carefully went down and cleared the hole. It is evident that this quintuple pot was the last object used in the ceremonies, and was thrown in on the top of all. A little way down, a long line of beads lay across the hole; another group-vase lay at the S.W. of the hole, formed of two vases with faces in relief on the necks, and a cow between the necks (XIV, 29). The objects had evidently been roughly cast into the pit, as the green glazed bowl, on the S.E., was broken up, and not all of it could be found; also the *menat* (XV, 75) was broken in two, the lower end lying eight inches north of the upper part, at the E. side of the hole. The string of beads and fish in glazed ware (XV, 75) attached to the *menat*, are in their original order, which was carefully traced when taking them from the earth. The scattered model eggs (62), in green glaze, balls (63), scarabs, etc., do not need remark, as they are numbered to correspond with the drawings.

Deposit 7 was in a pit about twenty inches deep. The forms of the vases are shewn sufficiently in the plan (PL. XVI), numbers marking those that are upright. The annex on the north-east was not open above, but was a hollow in the side of the circular pit to hold the smaller objects. In this hollow, and before it, lay the copper models of tools upon the floor of the pit; above them stood the alabaster vases (XIV, 4, 5), leaning inwards, around two pots, the outer almost cylindrical, the inner a saucer filled with lead ore. In the west of these was a piece of alabaster, shaped as a very thick saucer, and inscribed outside (XIV, 6). The vases were all likewise inscribed by incising them and filling the hollow with blue. The model corn-grinders (XIV, 1, 3) are of sandstone, and inscribed with blue paint. They lay confusedly in front of the recess, partly blocking the mouth of it, but are not drawn in the plan to avoid confusing it. One is marked at the S. of the deposit 7.

Although no deposit was found on the north side, yet under the foundations lay a broken figure of a cow in green glaze, with large black spots. It has lost the legs; the length is about 6 inches.

Probably of the same age as the deposits are two circular shallow pits, filled with a few inches of sand, on the S. side of the temple area (see under the letters Tahut*mes*). These are probably the foundations for column bases.

Of inscriptions of this age not much was recovered. A fragment of red granite bears the name of Tahutmes II (XIII, 1), probably from the throne of a statue. Of his son there are the great red granite pillars in the Coptic church (XXVI), the red granite jambs of a door (XIII, 5, 6), which were later inscribed by Osorhon (7). And three slabs of sculpture here figured (XIII, 2, 3, 4) probably belonged to this king. A relief of a king's head is most likely also of Tahutmes III (Manchester). Beside these we also found, of probably the same age, a lion's head of fine work in limestone (Univ. Coll.), which may have come from some early gargoyle of a temple; being in limestone, it looks as if it might be of Usertesen's time, and the workmanship would not be unsuited to that. A head of a life-size figure, which was found near the central Ptolemaic steps, represents some official of the time of Amenhotep III. (Manchester.)

25. Of the XIXth dynasty, the earliest evidence is the base of a small sandstone sphinx of Sety I; but the most important object was the great triad of life-size seated figures of Ramessu II between Isis and Hathor (PL. XVII). It is carved in dark brown-red granite of large grain. It lay on its back upon the northern flight of steps (Isis? steps), leading to the Ptolemaic temple. It had therefore been shifted in the rebuilding, and used as a decoration for the later temple. What position it occupied is not clear; but as the base was toward the south, it had probably stood on a pedestal between the pillars on the south of the steps. About a foot of earth was beneath it, so it had not been dragged down until the temple was in disuetude; probably the Theodosian decree had caused its fall. The face of Hathor had been knocked off, but nearly all of it was found lying at hand, and has been restored to its place. This group is the only large triad in the Ghizeh Museum, which entailed its being kept there. The photograph here was kindly taken by Brugsch Bey.

26. A portion of a stele of black quartzose stone was found close to the triad (PL. XVIII, 1). It has been engraved over an older inscription, a portion of which was found, having been broken off in re-dressing the block. This shews that the block was probably of the Middle Kingdom, and must have been, when complete, a very fine work; the hieroglyphs were less than half the size of the present ones, and the inscription must therefore have been very long. The unprincipled Ramessu had the whole of it erased and re-engraved with the present cutting, coarse in

work and inflated in style. Mr. Griffith translates it as follows:—

"(1) Ramessu mery-Amen, like the sun (2) . . . [the nobles of] every nation bringing their tribute of (3) . . . of much gold of much silver of every sort of mineral (4) . . . very many prisoners of Kesh-kesh (one of the Hittite allies), very many prisoners (5) . . . the writings of the king (User-maat-ra, sotep-en-ra) son of the sun (Ramessu mery-Amen) (6) . . . many flocks of goats, many flocks of she-goats, before his second daughter (7) . . . [bringing tribute] for (Ramessu) who gives life to Egypt for the second time. It was not the army that caused them to bring them, it was not . . . (8) . . . [it was the gods] of the land of Egypt, the gods of every country that caused the great princes of every country to bring (9) [them] themselves to the king (User-maat-ra, sotep-en-ra) son of the sun (Ramessu mery-Amen) giving life, (10) . . . to convey their gold, to convey their silver, to convey their vases of malachite (11) . . . [to the] son of the sun (Ramessu mery-Amen) giving life; to bring their herds of horses, to bring their herds of (12) [oxen, to bring their herds] of goats to bring their herds of sheep. It was the sons of the great princes of the land of the Khita (13) . . . that bore them themselves as far as the frontier of the lands of the king (User-maat-ra, sotep-en-ra) son of the sun (Ramessu mery-Amen) giving life, (14) . . . it was not a prince who went to fetch them, it was not an army of infantry that went to fetch them, it was not horsemen that went to fetch them, it was not (15) . . . [that went] to fetch them. It was Ptah father of the gods that placed all lands and all countries under the feet of this good god for ever and ever."

This inscription, from the style of it, appears to have been a hymn of praise to be recited. The idea of it, that all nations were compelled by the gods to bring tribute to Egypt, does not appear elsewhere.

The next large work of this reign is the stele with Ramessu and the sacred bark of Isis borne upon the priests' shoulders (PL. XIX, 1). Ramessu stands offering incense to "the elder Isis, mother of the god," "making incense offering to his mother Isis by her son Ramessu." The tablet appears to have been erected by the foreman of the building of the Ramesseum, Neb-nekht-tuf, who records his affairs below in eighteen columns of inscription as follows:—

"(1) The overseer of works in the temple of User-maat-ra, [Neb-nekht-tuf born of . . .] (2)-sekhet *makheru*, says, Adoration to thee Isis . . .

(3) fair of face in the Adtet boat, great of prowess . . . (4) ills, abolishing quarrels, driving away . . . (5) saving the weak from the fierce . . . (6) upon the ground Thy city . . . (7) . . . (8) me upon Egypt, I stood amongst . . . (9) the nobles as chief of the *mezay* . . . (10) this humble servant reached his city in order to give praise to Isis, to glorify [the great goddess] (11) every day. She stopped at this chief of the *mezay* . . . (12) she beckoned to him, she put me beside him I [adored her saying] (13) thou hast made Neb-nekht-tuf, thou wilt make . . . (14) . . . thou wilt cause . . . behold I made a tablet like unto it . . . (15) all her ways are established well, her hand is not stayed . . . (16) behold what was done to him was done to me : I officiated as governor of the foreigners in the north land, I officiated [as chief of] (17) the *mezay*, also as charioteer of his majesty and royal ambassador to every land ; overseer [of works in the] (18) temple of User-maat-ra, sotep-en-ra in the temple of Amen (i.e. Ramesseum) as a profitable servant like myself. Isis had given to me. . . ."

This stele was found a little east of the Usertesen door-jamb. It had therefore been shifted at the re-building of the Ptolemaic temple, as it was lying face down in the base sand. (Oxford.)

By the Isis steps was also found a large headdress of Ramessu II, of the usual Osiride form ; it must have belonged to a colossus of the king. (Manchester.) Another work of this period is a large baboon in black granite, with a pectoral on the breast shewing "the high priest of Amen Fua-mer, *makheru*," offering Maat to a seated figure of Tahuti. (Manchester.) The upper part of a rather rough tablet of sandstone, perhaps of this age, shews the Ba bird, with offerings before it, adoring the sun, which is passing into the mountains of the west : below was a scene of the 3rd prophet of Min, a scribe . . . and the divine father, a scribe . . . adoring Osiris. A part of a limestone tablet of rough work shews a bark borne by twelve priests, and having the collar at each end with a ram's head bearing a disc ; below is borne a similar sacred bark of Horus, with a hawk's head bearing a disc. There is no indication on the tablet, or at Koptos, to shew whether the ram represents Khnum, Hershafi, or some other god.

A block of Merenptah was found re-used in the Ptolemaic pavement on the south side of the area.

27. Of Ramessu III a granite stele was found (XVIII, 2) shewing the king offering to Min, Isis and Horus son of Isis, the earliest instance of the triad of Koptos which was so fixed in later times. In place of the sun's disc between the uraei and wings, is inserted "Messu heq An," i.e. Ramessu III. Five lines of inscription remain, reading " (1) Year 29 under the good god, the sun of Egypt, the prince of the lands of the gods, good heir of Hor-akhti, divine hawk (2) like Horus son of Isis, good disposer of all lands, whose method is established excellent like Tahuti lord of beauty (3) gracious to his suppliant . . . good of desire like Tum, the king, lord of both lands, (User-maat-ra, mery-Amen) son of the sun, lord of the crowns, (4) (Ramessu, heq An) abounding in possessions, intelligent concerning them, taste and daintiness (?) are with him like the goddess Urthekau (5) every land is moistened (?) by his *ka* and fears his majesty, abounding in captures, great in wondrous qualities, causing Egypt to rejoice . . ." Below this has probably been about as much more inscription, entirely scaled away owing to its having anciently stood where moisture reached it : no decay had taken place when it was entirely buried after the ruin of the temple. (Ghizeh Museum.) The lower parts of two baboons in sandstone also bore the name of Ramessu III. (Manchester.)

28. The upper part of a limestone stele of Isis, daughter of Ramessu VI (XIX, 2), was found at the back of the Ptolemaic temple, some-way east of the "Usertesen slab." It is important historically as shewing the name of the wife of Ramessu VI, *Nub-khesdeb*, "gold and lazuli," which has not been found before. In the middle is a dedication to "The Osiris, the king, lord of both lands (Maat-neb-ra, mery-Amen) son of the sun (Ramessu, Amen-her-khepshef, neter heq An) father of the divine wife of Amen (the adorer of the god, Isis)." On the right Isis offers to "Osiris . . . lord of the sacred land, great god, chief of Agert." She is "making a libation to Osiris the lord of eternity ; mayest thou grant me to receive food which is offered on thy tables, consisting of all good and pure things, from the Osiris the divine wife of Amen, the royal daughter, the lady of both lands, (the adorer of the god, Isis) *makheru*." Behind her is the name of " Her father, the king, lord of both lands (Maat-neb-ra, mery-Amen) son of the sun (Ramessu. . . .)" On the left side of the tablet the princess Isis offers to " Ra Har-akhti by whose beams the earth is enlightened, great god, prince of eternity." She says, " I play the sistrum before thy fair face, gold is in front of thee, grant that I may see the early dawn." Said by the Osiris the hereditary princess,

great of favours, the divine wife of Amen, the royal daughter, (the adorer of the god, Isis)." Her mother is "the great wife of the king, whom he loves, lady of both lands (Nub-khesdeb) *makheru*." (At Manchester.)

Of Ramesside work also is a part of a stele of a man adoring a prince of Koptos, Ankh-f-ma-ra son of Rames. On the back of this are traces of an inscription of another official, naming his offices under "the king mery-Amen Painezem," "renewed to him by his son his beloved, the high priest of Amen king of the gods . . . Masahart, *makheru*." (Univ. Coll.) One of the Osorkons added his name to the door-jambs of Tahutmes III (XIII, 7). Of Psamtek I or II one block has remained (XXVI, 1). A small chapel of Osiris, built by Aahmes Sineit, stood by the temenos to the south of the third pylon, in line with the south wall. Only the lower course, with ribbing of papyrus stems on it, remains *in situ ;* but a slab with a figure of Osiris was found in it. This had been re-stuccoed and painted a considerable time after it was first carved ; and hence it is more likely to belong to a permanent chapel of Osiris, than to be a place for the transient worship of some king.

Of the XXVIth dynasty also is a headless figure of a great official Horuza (XVIII, 3), carved in quartzite sandstone. It is finely wrought, the pebbles in the stone being smoothly cut through and polished : the hieroglyphs are well formed, in the taste of that age, as is also the symmetrical arrangement of the inscription. It reads "Oh prophets and priests that go up to Min and the gods of Koptos, as the gods of your city praise you, as ye make the festival of your king and fulfil your monthly services, as your children are in health, your houses in prosperity, your lands ordered, as ye pass on your offices to your sons, as ye love life and hate death :—so say ye, May the king give an offering, and Isis of Koptos, may she give a good burial and conveyance to the state of a favoured veteran, to the *ka* of the hereditary noble, prophet of the great cycle of gods, great seer of Heliopolis, Horuza ; and all funerary offerings to the *ka* of the pious servant of Horus lord of Koptos, ruler of nobles of the north and south, ruler of the palace, the great seer, Horuza." Here again Isis and Horus have superseded Min, as we have noticed in the Ramesside times.

The XXXth dynasty has left some trace here ; a fragment of a small obelisk of brown granite was carved under Nekht-hor-heb, by Aruerza (XXVI, 2). A similar name occurs in Mar. Cat. Abyd., 1240,

Turin stele, 159, and Paris Bib. Nat. (see Lieblein) ; and the name may possibly read Artierza or Mertierza. And a small chapel some distance to the south of the temple pylons, near the town wall, has a figure of Nekht-hor-heb, but seems from its work to be more probably of Ptolemy XIII and Augustus, whose names it also bears.

CHAPTER IV.

PTOLEMAIC AND ROMAN PERIOD.

30. We now reach the third great period of re-construction, which was more extensive than the work of either the Middle Kingdom or of Tahutmes III. We shall first review here the plan of the whole temple, which has never been subject to any later arrangement, and is therefore still visible in its main features ; though we cannot safely distinguish in many parts between the work of the earlier and later Ptolemies.

The temple itself appears to have been greatly enlarged. All over the area within the thick wall portions of a massive pavement of two courses of rough cut blocks were found in various parts. The " great pit " at the south side is a deep hollow in the basal yellow clay, five feet in depth, and with nearly vertical sides. It was probably the sacred lake or temple tank of pre-Ptolemaic times. In the Ptolemaic reconstruction a larger temple tank was provided a little way to the north of the temenos, where a deep hollow to below water-level still exists, and is filled with a varying pond, rising and falling with the Nile. This older "great pit" was filled up with clean sand like the whole temenos area in general, and covered with the uniform double pavement. The older sculptures which were lying still about the sacred site were put out of the way into all the hollows of the basal clay, and thus the three statues of Min, the slabs of Pepy, the vulture of Amenemhat, the stele of Rahotep, and other fragments, were all disposed of beneath the grand platform of sand and pavement which made a clear space for the Ptolemaic work. This sand-bed we turned over down to the basal clay, throughout the whole area within the temenos, except where later constructions of some height stood on it, and over part of the great pit, where the labour of shifting such a depth was very great. It might still be worth while to clear out all the great pit ; but until

D

the plans were completed I did not fully realise its nature. The foundations of buildings which we left unmoved were generally searched by undermining, to see if sculptured blocks were employed in them; and in this way we found some of the finest work, that of the scenes of Amenemhat I and Usertesen I (PL. IX), placed face down at the bottom of the later foundations.

This rearrangement of Ptolemaic times is of much interest, as hitherto we have known nothing of what became of the older remains of the great sites, such as Dendera, Esneh, and Edfu, which are to all present appearance purely Ptolemaic. The Dendera of Khufu lies probably in pits beneath the sand-bed of the foundations of the great temple of the Ptolemies and Romans: and the sculptures of the magnificent work of the XIIth dynasty might be looked for on the under sides of the lowest foundations of Edfu.

The limits of the Ptolemaic platform of pavement were fully built up to on the north: and there I found the foundation deposits beneath the high wall-courses on the pavement. But on the south I could not find any deposits at the corners, perhaps because the buildings did not extend over the pavement to the limits. At the back of the temple an open unpaved space was left in the temenos; and from that a gateway led out to the north, so much decayed that I could not trace its exact limits between the mud filling of it and the mud bricks of the wall. At the south-east corner also the brickwork could not be traced continuously to the south side, and hence there was probably a small gate there. The difficulty of making certain whether a cutting is made in wall or washed mud, is considerable when the soil is moist, the depth such that wide clearances at one time are out of the question, and the bricks so pressed and contorted that scarcely any trace of structure can be seen in the wall.

Over the whole space to the east of the Tahutmes temple lay a confused mass of shifted blocks and fallen architraves of the Ptolemaic and Roman periods. The pieces were too much broken, and too seldom connected in character, for any restoration of the structure to be possible. From a fragment of a Hathor head it appears that there were columns of that type, about two-thirds the size of those at Dendera. The sizes of the architraves were 41 inches (2 cubits) square, and also 52 and 53 inches (2½ cubits) square. They were sculptured with inscriptions, of which the most continuous portions are copied on PL. XXVI. Fragments of columns at the front shew a diameter of 90 inches; others in the middle shew 68 inches. It is evident, therefore, that the Ptolemaic temple extended to the east, and had its most important parts quite off the site of the earlier sanctuary.

31. In the front we gain some indication of its arrangements. A long stone basement remains on the west, divided by three flights of stone steps. These were all contemporary, as they stand equally related in position to the one stone wall. And it seems not too much to suppose that they led to three separate shrines in the temple, like the double entrance of Ombos. The different gods of the well-known triad of Koptos—Min, Isis, and Horus—in later times, might be connected with these three entrances. And as on the northern staircase the group of Ramessu with Isis and Hathor was found—as the tablet of the bark of Isis lay on the same northern side, about east of the Usertesen jamb—as the sculptures on the curtain wall between the columns north of the northern steps shew only Isis—and as the inscription on the pylon before that (PL. XXII) names the temple of Isis—it seems fairly certain that the northern stairway led to the Isis shrine. Of the other two stairways there is not much evidence of their purpose. But as there is shewn on a tablet of Roman age (XXII, 2) a shrine of Min as the great object of the place, it is more likely that the great steps in the main axis of the whole place belong to Min, and the lesser steps to Horus. Before the temple were two series of pylons, those of Isis and those of Min. The only one bearing sculpture was the innermost pylon of Isis, which had a long inscription on the east wall of the gate-keeper's recess (PL. XXII, 1); on the north wall of the same recess is a scene of Min with the king behind him, and the queen, Nebhat, Sekhet, and Nut before him: and on the wall between the recess and the Isis steps are figures offering, a king and a Nile figure. Lying by this pylon was a fragment of the Greek dedication (PL. XXII, 2):

ΤΠΕΡ ΒΑΣΙΛ[ΕΩΣ ΠΤΟΛΕΜΑΙΟΤ . . . .]
ΠΡΟΠΤΛΟ[Ν . . . .]

The only other case in which a propylon is named in a dedication is at Dendera, under Augustus (Letronne, Rec. Ins., p. 81, pl. V, F; Mariette, Dendera, p. 32); and this inscription is very probably of Ptolemy XIII. Of the other pylons only the foundations or lower parts of the walls remain. The great entrance pylon was cleared down to the basal clay at its corners, in search of deposits. The course joints were at 0, 18,

28, 46, and 78 inches, there being four courses of rough-cut foundation remaining. The great brick wall in which this gate is, forms part of the main fortification of Roman times, having semi-circular bastions along it on the other three sides, and containing nearly all the town of Koptos.

32. The foundation deposits were found under the two northern corners of the Ptolemaic building. After I had obtained a clue to the plan of the place, I then dug deep wells down at the corners, to follow the wall and reach into the foundation sand. The men grumbled at making such deep holes, but were astounded when I went down, and after a few minutes' scraping in the sand took out the gilt blocks of stone (XXIII, 5). The story went round the town that I could tell exactly where the treasure was buried, set a man to dig down deep in the earth close to it, and then go and take out all the gold with my own hands. It certainly had more substance in it than most oriental tales.

The plans of these two deposits are given, PL. XVI at bottom. It does not appear that there was any system in placing them : the distance from the corner of the stone (shewn in the plan) is not the same, nor the positions of the pieces. The figures upon the objects shew the depth of them in inches under the lowest stone ; they vary from nine to three inches down. The numbers outside of the objects shew the nature of them, referring to the numbers in PL. XXIII. On that plate are shewn the various materials and forms: the gold is represented by gilt blocks of sandstone, the silver was a plating over a piece of wood, which is now rotted away, the bronze and lead are solid blocks ; the glass is mainly decomposed, while the pieces of ore and stone are as when buried. The alabaster pieces from the two corners fitted together. The vases were all of the forms here shewn, mostly of the smaller size. The cartouches were all written with ink, and only traces remain on the lead and yellow glass. The form does not agree to any of the variants known of any Ptolemaic name.

At the bottom of this plate are two blocks of limestone, painted blue, found under foundation at the east end of the temple. Also a square tile of white inlaid with blue glaze, probably of early Naukratite work, which was found in the town.

33. Turning now to the other remains which do not involve the architecture, we see first a scene on the curtain wall, or screen, between the eastern pair of columns, north of the Isis steps. This whole scene of fifteen blocks was transported to England and is now at Oxford. Is was needful to remove it, as the natives began to pull it down for the sake of the blocks bearing faces, for sale to dealers. The scene represents Ptolemy I deified, standing before a shrine receiving offering of incense from a priest ; behind the priest are six standards, the Ibis, one defaced, the Hawk, the piece of flesh (?), the jackal, and the Min sign with two plumes ; and beyond these stands " the great Isis princess of all the gods." This scene was at a lower level than the top of the steps, so it appears that after the building under Philadelphos, the floor of the temple was raised and the steps heightened probably under Ptolemy XIII Dionysos. This accounts for the Isis steps intruding beyond the line of the front wall.

34. The most important inscription of the Greek age is of the reign of Philadelphos (PL. XX). It is carved minutely and very regularly upon a large thin slab of basalt ; from the fracture of one edge it seems probable that this was a sheet of background behind a statue, such as we see behind the figures of Ty and Ranefer in the Ghizeh Museum. The slab was kept at that museum, as a small piece of it had been previously acquired there. What I found was lying re-used as a floor stone in a brick building in the S.W. corner of the plan PL. I. The inscription is translated by Mr. Griffith as follows :—

"(1) . . . his boundaries thereto between the two seas (Mediterranean and Red Sea). (2) . . . his beauties shine in every face, even as the sun illumines the day. He is as . . . (3) . . . with plumes like his father Min of Koptos, the king of Upper and Lower Egypt, loved of the two lands (User-ka-ra, mery-Amen), son of the sun, lord of the diadems [Ptelumys . . . (4) . . . the hereditary noble, the sole companion] the noble at the head of the people, great in his office, high in his dignity, advanced in position in the palace, on whose utterance the king relies, to whom are told the proceedings of . . . (5) . . . the greatest dignitary from the two lands, the officer standing on the (king's) right hand, ready of speech, loving the council-chamber of difficult questions, discussing the teachings of the good god, praised by the king . . . (6) . . . turning his face to his adviser, his back upon the evil . . . (7) . . . beloved of the lord of this land, preparing the the way that he desires, protecting the city of Koptos, defending its nome, a place of retreat behind the estates (?), strong in smiting, remembering him who remembers him, chief of the living, by whose advice are regulated the affairs of the palace . . . (8) . . . right and left of the child of intelligence to produce pleasantness of discourse, floating on the current of the gods, but to prevent the speaker from delay in dalliance. A man with mind present in an unprecedented moment. He made him to find methods . . . [the whole land] (9) prayed for his health day and night in matters pertaining to his decision; a mooring-post for him who is swept away (?) a raft (?) for the drowning man, relieving him who is suffocated. The oppressed cried to him . . . protecting their bodies from every ill . . . (10) protecting the aged, guarding the guardians, punishing greed toward the defenceless, a man of arithmetic, a very Thoth in accuracy, knowing what reports are like (?). Many said " Beauty beside him there is none " (?) a man of frankincense, loving the wine-cup, gracious of eyes on the day of . . . (11) skilled in writing, a man to whom comprehension came swiftly (?) satisfying the heart of his master, superintendent of the royal *harim*, chief officer of his majesty, chief of the servants of the princess, the great favourite, mistress of the two lands, pleasing the heart, gracious and sweet of love, fair of crowns, receiving the two diadems, filling the palace with her beauties, the principal royal wife, pacifying the heart of the king of Upper and Lower Egypt, lord of both lands (User-ka-ra, mery-Amen), son of the sun, lord of the diadems (Ptelumys) . . . (12) priest of Osiris, Horus, and Isis of *Het-zefau* and the gods of *Het-zefau*, of Isis the image in the nome of Koptos, of the lion of the south and the lion of the north, of Shu and Tefnut, the son and daughter of Ra in Qus, of the elder Isis mother of the god on the great throne of Osiris in the shrine, of Ptah Sokar Osiris the great god in the sarcophagus of Osiris of Koptos in Het-nub, Senu-sher-sheps."

(Hymn to Min.)

" (13) He says before his master, Glory to thee . . . Min of Koptos, Horus raising the arm, great of love, piercing the sky with his double plume, lord of joy in the shrine, king of the gods, sweet of love, full of his mother, upon his great throne, great god in the two hemispheres, in Hesep, surmounting his staircase, purifying (?) the flesh of god, offering to his father, male of the gods, valiant in . . . (14) . . . prince of the desert, loving mankind he has created youths. His abomination is to say 'Cut short the breath of life by which one lives;' causing to breathe him who follows his current. Fair of face, he enriches the two breasts, beautiful beyond the gods, his excellence is beyond the divine cycle, satisfying the majesty in the

desert and in the eastern mountains . . . (15) . . . travelling upon his current, healing the sick, making the distressed to live, good physician (?) to him that puts him in his heart, making to live him whose heart is contracted. I am thy servant, travelling upon thy current, thou has founded (?) my heart in the egg, lest precious stones should be scattered (?) . . . (16) . . . thy great city. I repeated for it the sealing of all its property by calculation. I slept not at night, I rested not in the daytime, searching after thy beauties in my heart.

(Deeds of Senu-sher.)

" When I found *Het-zefau* gone to ruin, worn . . . (17) . . . [I removed] the mud (?) I built a wall around it for the second time, the length 110 cubits, the breadth 40 cubits, the depth 15 cubits. I dug the ground to make a channel of 6 cubits in order to raise the floor in the whole temple. I built . . . (18) . . . sistrum, . . . their clappers (?) of bronze engraved with the great name of his majesty. I made all his utensils of bronze, though I found not such things of former workmanship. I enlarged his house with all good things: I provisioned his altars, I increased his offerings in the offering-place, I established . . . (19) . . . a gateway of good white living stone, its length 15 cubits, breadth 6 cubits to the top of the hinges (?) around (?) its entrance (?) inscribed with the great name of his majesty; its doors of cedar (?) overlaid with bronze, its hinges of bronze of Setet. The pylon-tower on the north built of brick for the dromos of Isis . . . (20) . . . the pylon of brick. I made a shrine of basalt for Horus Isis and Osiris upon the great throne, the great god in his shrine. I renewed the monuments in the house of Osiris . . . (21) . . . mayest thou prolong my existence upon earth (?) . . . growing old, resting in the good necropolis in the nome of Koptos . . . [to the ka of].

Column 1 " . . . the nome of Koptos in the sacred places of the queen: making to reign the mistress of the villages and districts in the southern Neter (parallel to the northern Neter, another town of Isis, now Behbit), accomplishing the heart's desire in all good work in hard stone and living rock, setting up statues of the king, lord of both lands (User-ka-ra mery-Amen), son of the sun, lord of the crowns (Pdelumeys), ever-living, and images of the queen. Never was the like done except by my Master in this land . . . festivals of the lord of both lands

(User-ka-ra mery-Amen), son of the sun, lord of the crowns, (Ptelum . . .) . . . (2) . . . (men will say) in finding his name in southern Neter, 'Let us come to you and tell you my good success; praise ye god for him who did service (?) without ceasing.' Give ye to me bread and beer, oxen and birds, wine and milk, incense and water, and all good and pure things sweet and pleasing that appear upon the altar of the elder Isis, mother of the god; of . . . daily, day and night; for I am a great one . . . (3) . . . making the weak and motherless to live, wall of life protecting his name, Senu-sher-sheps, the superintendent of the royal *harim* of Arsynifau (Arsinoe), the chief royal wife of the king, lord of both lands (User-ka-ra mery-Amen), son of the sun, lord of the crowns (Pdelumys), ever-living. He says, Oh! every eye that seeth the sun, the circuit made by Tum, and every one that cometh . . . (4) (on the edge). [*Seten du hotep* to Osiris] to Har-pe-khroti, the very great, chief child of Amen (see Br. Geog. 831), and to the gods and goddess who are in the southern Neter, may they give offerings of oxen, cranes, and all things good, pure, sweet and pleasant, for the hereditary noble, the royal sealbearer, the sole companion, Senu-sher-sheps. . . ."

Mr. Griffith remarks that the name of the writer is Senu-sher or Senu-sher-sheps, the latter form being clear in the third column. His principal function was that of *major-domo* of a queen of Ptolemy Philadelphos, named Arsinoe. There can be no doubt that this was not his favourite wife and sister Arsinoe, whom he married in middle life (B.C. 279), but the daughter of Lysimachus of Thrace, and the mother of his successor; he had married her (B.C. 285), in early life, but banished her to Koptos for fictitious or real intrigues of one sort or another. If historians are to be trusted, the banishment of his first wife, and the marriage with his sister, took place very soon after his accession, so that his first wife must have been already in exile at Koptos when this inscription was cut. She still, however, bore most flowery titles, and was evidently treated as a royal personage. Her name is peculiarly rendered in hieroglyphics, as if to distinguish her from her rival, and she is not named royal sister.

The ex-queen appears to have had a district in the region of Koptos assigned to her, named the southern Neter (the northern Neter or Iseum—now Behbit el Hagar—being another great centre of Isis worship like Koptos), and her statues were erected by her *major-domo* side by side with those of her recent husband. She must therefore have had something like absolute authority in this petty kingdom assigned to her.

Senu-sher held important priesthoods in the Osiride temple of Koptos, but apparently not in the shrine of Min, although he gives here a long hymn to Min. The same separation appears in the Ptolemaic story of Setna, several scenes of which are laid in Koptos, but which makes no mention of Min, while the priests of Isis and Harpokrates figure in it frequently.

35. The dimensions which are here recorded for the Philadelphian rebuilding were eagerly compared with the plan so soon as I found the inscription at Koptos. The length agrees well enough with the total from the front wall to the outside of the back of the temenos; according to the plan, this varies from 4445 to 4455 inches, which is equal to 110 double cubits of 40·4 to 40·5 inches. But the breadth of the temenos as it now stands, is more like 70 than 40 double cubits; the only possible reckoning as 40 would be taking only the stone building, and supposing that the earlier Ptolemaic temple was symmetrical about the Tahutmes temple, and that the expansion on one side to the south beyond the great pit is due to the Dionysian reconstruction. But the obvious difficulty in this is that the 110 cubits of length include the thick brick wall, and the dimensions are stated to be those of a wall around the temple, and must therefore include the wall in the breadth. It might be then better to refer the dimensions to a stone wall, like that of Edfu, around the temple, inside of the brick wall; and suppose the length to extend from the front of the third pylon to the back foundation deposit, and the breadth from the northern foundation deposit to a wall near the site of the vulture, symmetrical about the Tahutmes temple. This view seems reasonable, and presents no serious difficulty. As the stone circuit wall of Edfu is over 20 cubits high, this wall being 15 cubits high would be quite probable. And the whole space of the temple of Koptos would then be a little longer and not quite so wide as that of Edfu (without the peristyle court), or Dendera. The fragments of columns indicate that those in the front and in the middle were slightly larger than the similar ones at Dendera (90 and 68, against 87 and 64 inches).

36. The large headdress in white marble (XXVI, 3) probably belonged to a statue of Arsinoe II, the second wife of Philadelphos, as the titles are fuller

than those of later queens ; there is no royal-mother title, which often occurs later, and it has exactly the same titles in the first column as those of Arsinoe I. That it is not the statue of Arsinoe I, named by Senu-sher, is shewn by the titles royal daughter and royal sister, which were not borne by the earlier queen. This block was found in the front court between the second and third pylon of Isis ; it is now at University College.

The next monument is the middle of a limestone statue of Ptolemy III Euergetes which has his name on the back of it (XXVI, 3 A) ; now at Manchester. The name of Ptolemy IX was observed on a block of granite which had been cut up for a mill-stone ; and after that we come to a considerable rebuilding under Ptolemy XIII (of Lepsius) Neos Dionysos. Several pieces of inscription of his occur on blocks in the temple (XXVI, 4, 5, 10) and a large cubical altar of black basalt covered with his inscriptions has been lying in the ruins, visible for many years.

A sandstone statue of apparently Ptolemaic age was found lying near the eastern wall of the temenos. The head is passably cut, and well-formed ; it wears a wreath of leaves, and a band of rosettes ; the dress is a long robe of which the tagged edge is held by the left hand in front ; the head was broken from the body, and the feet are lost. (Philadelphia.) A large lion-head gargoyle was probably belonging to the outer wall of the temple ; it lay by the Min steps. This, and a piece of an elaborate capital of Roman age, are in South Kensington Museum.

37. Under the earlier emperors a good deal of activity appears here. The small chapel south of the temple bears the name of Augustus. The temple building begun by Ptolemy XIII, (about 56 B.C.) was continued by Tiberius (see XXVI, 6, 7, 8) and Nero (XXVI, 9) ; many of the architraves and other blocks about the eastern end are of this age, by their style, and they shew that a building quite comparable to the shrines of Esneh or of Dendera had stood here ; and fragments seen in modern use bear the names of Caligula and Claudius. What cause can have led to such a wholesale clearance of sandstone from here, while it remains untouched in places north and south of this, is difficult to understand. But with Nero the history of the temple, as such, comes to a close.

Turning to the remainder of the Egyptian inscriptions, there was found outside the temenos to the north-west, a sandstone stele of Tiberius adoring Horus and Isis, with an inscription in hieroglyphics and demotic. This lay face down for paving ; now

in the Ghizeh Museum. Another sandstone stele is rougher in style, but bears an interesting subject, (XXII, 3). An emperor, apparently Nero, is offering to Min, who stands with the usual attributes, while behind him is a shrine with a long sloping ascent and a figure in it holding a spear. This figure is not that of Min, as the arm does not bear a whip, and it wears a wig. It seems rather to be Horus, with his spear for slaying the crocodile, the avenger of his father, as shewn at Edfu. The inscription in hieroglyph is " Live Horus, the warrior, smiting the foreign countries, Nero Cæsar (?) : he has made his monument to his father Min-Ra . . . the land in Het-shau : may he live like Ra for ever." Below this, in demotic, is " Before Min the image the great god . . . Perthonius (?) son of Pamin whose mother is Khuy . . . for ever . . . Nero Claudius Cæsar, Augustus, Germanicus, Imperator." *Het-shau,* " house of sand," must be the name of a temple or shrine in Koptos not otherwise known, probably the shrine which is here represented.

38. The later history of Koptos is illustrated by the Greek and Latin inscriptions, which are fully described and discussed by Mr. Hogarth in the last chapter. Here we may note their historical positions. After the hieroglyphic inscriptions of Tiberius and Nero, we see that some public work went on here under Galba, the inscription of which remained (XXVIII, 2). Under Domitian the bridge over the canal was rebuilt from the foundation ; and the inscription of this work, which is one of the very rare examples of Latin in Egypt (XXVIII, 3), was afterwards taken into the town, and broken in two for building stone. A native digger found it, and sold it to me. The great tariff inscription was found shortly before I arrived at Koptos, and had been secured by the native guardian belonging to the museum. The place of it was in a little dusty rise of soil in the middle of the two-mile belt of cultivation between Koptos and the desert. The present dyke-road in crossing the plain winds someway to the south of this hillock ; but it seems probable that this site was on the ancient road, as it lies exactly between the Roman town and the present head of the road when it joins the desert. The road then probably ran straight past this toll-gate, and has been diverted up stream by continual patching and repairs of breaches in the dyke. The entry for a funeral up to the desert and back was a most tantalizing item ; we were searching for the cemetery, and this seemed to prove that it was on the desert ; yet though we

examined every likely position for some miles, we did not succeed: and we were forced to conclude that this tax referred to a comparatively small Roman cemetery on the edge of the desert by the road. The cemetery of Koptos is referred to in the tale of Setna in such a way as to imply that it adjoined the town; and it seems possible that it may have been upon a part of the clay island which has since been entirely covered over by the rising deposits of the Nile.

After this there is one inscription known of Antoninus, dated under the Eparch Lucius Munatius Felix (Rec. XVI, 44); a brief dedication on a column is dated in the reign of Severus (XXVIII, 5): and a most interesting altar belongs to the reign of Caracalla (XXVIII, 6). The god Ierablos, from whom the city was named, is an obvious new point; but it was not till Prof. Sayce was looking over it that the Baal Akabos or Yakub was cleared up by him. It is seldom that two such contributions to mythology are given by one short inscription. I found the stone built in as the threshold of the door of a peasant's house, and at once bought it. Of Caracalla also the unusual monument was found of a colossal head of the emperor in red granite. It lay on the steps of the Isis temple, and shews therefore that a statue had been erected by the entrance to the temple, and that therefore the building was still in repair and in use at that date. The likeness of the portrait is unmistakable, and the work is probably due to a Greek artist of the time, as there is nothing Egyptian in the style of it. (Now at Philadelphia.)

The next fixed point is in the inscription of Quietus (XXVIII, 7) about 260 A.D.; and it should be noted how in this and others of the Greek inscriptions (as 6 and 12) the influence of the tall Latin script, with cross bars at the ends of the strokes, is obvious. It shews that Latin was more familiar than Greek writing to those who set the style, and reflects the importance of the Roman garrison at Koptos.

The latest inscription known from Koptos is one at the Ghizeh Museum (Rec. XVI, 44.). It is dated in the 627th year of an era, which can hardly be other than the Seleucid era. It appears strange to find this era used in Egypt, but as the dedication is in honour of certain messengers from Emesa in Syria, it is not an unlikely compliment to them. The date would then be 315 A.D.; and this agrees well with another point. The Praepositus of the Gallic legion here is named Victorinus; he would be almost certainly so called after Victorinus the usurper in

Gaul, 265–267 A.D. His age in an important office would probably be between 40 and 60, and this would bring us to between 305 and 325 A.D., which just agrees with the dating by the Seleucid era. The inscription is not very correctly published, but after some emendations (such as Arabarch in l. 3, Africae in l. 5, &c.) it appears to read thus:—"Dedicated on behalf of the Emesian messengers. With the consent of the High Priest of Dionysos, on the good day . . . the Arabarch dedicated this for the good fortune of the messengers from Emesa. And for the welfare of the Vexillation of the Gallic legion and the Ala Africae under the Praepositus Victorinus, year 627, month Lous 15."

This Ala Secunda Ulpia Afrorum was at the north-eastern frontier of Egypt in the following century, according to the Notitia. This dedication closes the series of the inscriptions of Koptos.

CHAPTER V.

THE MINOR ANTIQUITIES.

39. For convenience of reference we will first notice those objects which are figured in the plates, in their numbered order. The foundation deposits have all been noticed in describing their respective temples.

XXI, 1. A piece of black steatite cup, with scroll border on the flat edge: found in the town. From the style of the scroll probably of the XIIth, or XVIIIth dynasty at the latest.

2. A piece of black steatite cup incised with a group of two goats browsing on a bush. A similar subject occurs incised on black pottery at Kahun (Kahun, XXVII. 200), and indicates that this steatite cup is probably of the XIIth dynasty. From the town.

3. A piece of a large alabaster vase with a narrow neck; inscribed with the name of Khufu, and the determinative of the seated king like that in the graffito of Seneferu (Medum, XXXII, 1). This was found low down in the town south of the temple; it was doubtless part of the furniture of the temple of Khufu. (F. P. coll.)

4, 5, 6. Three bronze standards in the form of a decorated lance. On 4 is a royal sphinx, and a figure of Horus binding the crocodile. On 5 is a hawk. On 6 is a hawk-head end to the lance, and Horus binding the crocodile. From the lance-head form and the hawk-head it might be at first supposed that these referred to Mentu ; but the evident figure of Horus and the crocodile, and their being found at Koptos, points to their belonging to Horus. The lance therefore must be of Horus, the avenger of his father ; though very probably the symbolism has been much influenced by the neighbourhood of the war-god Mentu.

7. A head in limestone of early style, perhaps of the Old Kingdom.

8. A bronze Lepidotus.

9. Piece of limestone tablet with the ram of Amen.

10. Back of an Osiris statue in limestone.

11–18. The Osiris figures of the XXVIth dynasty and onward are very numerous ; and they illustrate the continued degradation by cheap imitation. The earlier ones are of fair work, in black steatite, yellow limestone, or cast bronze : the example in steatite (11) was dedicated by Khonsu-pa-āua son of Amen-du-nekht and Ast-khebt (bought at Koptos, F. P. Coll.). A fine head in thinly cast bronze on an ash core, of about the same scale, was found in the temple near the great pit. (Manchester.) Then come figures on a lesser scale (12), without any dedication, but of fair work. Next these were made slight and more conventional, cast shrunken and solid, without any ash core, as 13. Then to save trouble the moulds were made conjoined, as in 14, so that many could be made at a single filling. The feet being narrower than the shoulders, they were made nearer together (15). And then degraded, as in 16, 17, and lastly 18, where they become a sort of radiating ornament, which we took them for at first sight. The only purpose of this long degradation, until the Osiris becomes vestigial, must have been economy in presenting them ; and as a single one of the type 18 cannot have been thought worth troubling about, it seems likely that there was a custom of vowing so many statues to Osiris, and we see here the means for dedicating a few hundreds without impoverishing the devotee.

19. A block of sandstone with a flight of steps in front, and a hollow shaped as a foot at the top. Several blocks of stone with marks of feet were found in the temple ; and they suggest that there was a sacred footprint here—as in so many countries at the present time—and that copies or models of it were made as *objets de piété*.

XXIV, XXV. Of scarabs a large number were found or bought at Koptos, but very few of importance. They are all figured here, as it is very desirable to shew what styles belong to each district. Those with names are as follows :—1, Amenemhat III ; 2,

Usertesen ; 3, Ay, Mer-nefer-ra ; 4, the Lady Uazit-hotep, daughter of Nem-mest ; 5, a royal priest ; 6, the artist and follower, Netrihotep ; 7, Ra-nefer ; 8, Apepa, Aa-seuser-ra ; 9, Sebakhotep III, probably of later date from the style of it, which is most like the scarabs of the XXVth dynasty ; 10–32, Tahutmes III ; 33, Tahutmes IV ; 35, Amenhotep IV ; 36, Sety I ; 37–38, Ramessu II ; 39, Ramesside ; 40, Shabaka, with the ram's head on the beetle, characteristic of the XXVth dynasty ; 41, Rameny, perhaps a vassal of Piankhy. The cylinder 42 is of a curious style, probably very early ; it is roughly cut in limestone, now burnt, and was found in the low-level town south of the temple. The other scarabs do not call for any special notice.

40. Turning now to the objects which are not figured, the earliest is probably a portion of a silver feather from a headdress of Min, $3\frac{1}{2}$ inches wide and 11 or 12 inches high, now broken to $9\frac{1}{2}$ inches, It was found low down in the soil of the southern side of the temple, in the Min region. A lower portion of a plant (or palm spathe ?), such as is seen behind Min on the sculptures, was found, made of green glaze marked out with blue, about 3 inches wide and 6 long ; this doubtless came from the fittings of a statue of Min, as also a fragment of a coffer in limestone, such as is represented behind statues of Min. (All in Univ. Coll.) Another fragment from temple fittings is a reed from a *sekhet* sign, in green glaze ; probably from a group where a king was offering fields to the god.

Portions of several window-gratings of sandstone were found on the temple site. Hitherto only the plain grid of vertical bars has been seen in temples, (Karnak, Ramesseum, and decorated in Deir el Medineh) ; but we have five other designs at Koptos. (1) Vertical bars having a curved slit above them, adapted to a round-headed window ; (2) lattice of bars crossing at about 55°, broken into panels by half-round columns between ; (3) dividing the surface into squares, the half of each square cut diagonally is perforated ; (4) a square panel perforated with a six-leaved rosette ; (5) an upright opening with a modified *ankh* of stone left in it. All of these are now at University College.

41. A curious series of small tanks of stone was found about the temple. Several of them have little stairways cut down the inner sides, and in one there are 14 steps on each of two opposite sides. These recall the stairway of 14 steps ascending and 14 steps descending which is mentioned at Koptos, and has evidently a lunar connection with the waxing and

waning moon. This tank gives a further view that these steps were at the great temple tank or sacred lake, and were copied in the model tanks provided in the temple. Why such model tanks were made may be gleaned from some details. They are all rough below and round the lower half, but finished smooth round the edge and inside. They were therefore not for dedications, to place free-standing in the temple, but must have been sunk half in the earth. The use of them is shewn by a foot carved in the bottom of one; they were probably for washing the feet before prayers in the temple, like the Islamic ablutions. And they were apparently thus used to save the trouble and unpleasantness of going down to the great tank, with the populace. Some persons were even more particular, and declined to use a model tank in common. One Aristius Saturninus, more fastidious or litigious than other people, had a tank solely for his own use, inscribed as his own place (XXVIII, 13).

In the town we found a trachyte corn-grinder, formed as a slab 16 × 11 inches and 3 thick, with a slit 9 × 1½ along the middle, and sloping sides to the slit, which has a sharp edge. Thus the corn was laid in the wide space over the slit, and gradually worked down through the slit as the stone was slid to and fro on a lower slab. Pieces of such are often found on Roman sites in the Delta ("Nebesheh," p. 27); and though at first mistaken for window-slits, the real use has been surmised, although a whole example has not been found before. In this instance, the bar-holes for fastening a cross handle for pushing it to and fro are unmistakable.

42. Of Roman age also is a fine brick tomb (XXVI, top), outside of the Roman fortification on the east. It has been preserved to a height of 9 feet 8 inches, by being deeply heaped around with broken pottery and rubbish of the third century A.D.; and these heaps have undergone slow combustion of the organic matter in them, which has baked them and the tomb to a brick-red colour. The dividing of the outside surface by pilasters, is akin to the so-called "Tomb of Absalom" at Jerusalem; and as this tomb cannot be later than the Antonines (by the date of the heaps which bury it), it is probably of the 1st or early 2nd century, A.D. Very probably the type was brought in by the Palmyrene archers stationed here, who were familiar with it in their own city. The interior is divided in two parts by a cross wall; and the access is by a doorway at either end in the upper storey. Probably the lower chambers contained the burial, as we found in them a large jar of blue glaze,

14½ inches high, which contained calcined bones. Over the lower part a brick floor was probably built, and the openings above may have had statues placed in them. Had they been closed as doors, the brick filling would probably have remained. The capitals of the pilasters had no detail, but were simply formed by projecting the bricks and smoothing the form to a rough moulding. Of Roman age is a curious stele of Osiris (V, 12), in which he is figured with the long cloak, six stars around him, Hor-sam-taui on one side, and the eye of Horus on the opposite side. (Ghizeh Museum.)

Of Roman remains many varieties of cups with white slip in high relief were found (in Brit. Mus., Roman), and other small objects which do not call for remark.

43. Of Coptic times is a stele with a doorway represented, much like Gayet, Fig. 24; but in this case there is an outer doorway of twisted columns supporting a pediment. (Univ. Coll.) The remains of a Coptic church (XXVI, top) stand between the ancient and modern town. The plan of it cannot now be traced, except in the region of the Baptistery, which is valuable as probably the oldest oriental baptistery remaining. The cruciform tank has three steps leading down into it: the central space is about 7 feet across between the parallel sides, affording plenty of space for immersion of adults, while the three recesses, being 28 inches wide, are fully sufficient for a person to stand in: possibly they were for the priest, and two deacons with the oil of exorcism and the oil of thanksgiving, in an earlier form of the ritual than now exists, when adult baptism was general. There are two pillars of red granite (taken from the temple of Tahutmes III) on the east of the tank, and a fallen one on the west, suggesting that a square canopy or baldachino stood over it. Two similar pillars are in the hall on the west. The scenes have been erased from nearly all the sides of these pillars, one being left untouched on the south side of the south pillar in the hall; the inscriptions are also erased, except that the *ankh* has been left intact, probably as a symbol of life or a form of the cross. Beside these there are some octagonal columns with circular bases, lying by the tank; these are of late Roman work. The remains of the capitals of limestone are of a debased Corinthian style, probably of the late IVth or the Vth century. If the interwoven capitals of Justinian extended so far, we could date this building certainly before his time; but common as they are at Constantinople, Ravenna and Jerusalem,

E

I do not know of an example south of St. Mark's at Alexandria (Gayet, p. 13). The foundations are built with blocks of the Ptolemaic and Roman temple.

44. It only remains to mention the various minerals found in the ruins; from the nearness to the eastern mountains an unusual variety occurs here, Quartz, crystal and milky, Hornstone, red Jasper, green Jasper Breccia, Beryl, Mica, Actinolite, Obsidian, Pumice, Steatite, Red Granite, White Granite, Red, Green and Gray Porphyry, Slate, Calcite, Lime Breccia, Red Haematite, Red Ochre, Iron Slag, Chrysocolla, Sulphide of Copper, and Realgar; beside Red and White Coral.

CHAPTER VI.

THE CLASSICAL INSCRIPTIONS.

By D. G. HOGARTH, M.A.

No. I.

. . . . . Θ]εῷ μεγίστῳ
. . . . .]μο[ς προσ]τάτης
. . . . . .] Θεᾶς Ἴσιδος
. . . .] μεσορὴ ἐπαγ(ομένων) αʹ.

45. On a block of black basalt, now in University College, London.

To . . . most high god . . . mus, steward of the . . . goddess Isis . . . in the month Mesori (July—August) on the 1st of the intercalated days dedicates this.

The style of the lettering, and the presence of *iota adscript*, suggest the late Ptolemaic period. The year was perhaps inscribed in the lost portion of l. 4. For the intercalated days, see C. I. G. 4879, 4825, etc., etc.

The name of the god cannot be supplied with any certainty, but it was probably a short name, for neither in l. 3 nor l. 4 does much seem to be lost. Perhaps the god was Pan = Min of Coptos.

The title προστάτης is found not infrequently. Cf. C. I. G. 4711, 4714; and Boeckh's introduction to Egyptian inscriptions, *Ibid.*, vol. iii.

No. II.

(Ἔτους) βʹ Σε(ρ)ουίου Γαλβᾶ Αὐτοκράτορος
Καίσαρος Σεβαστοῦ
μηνὸς νέου σεβαστοῦ
καʹ.

46. On a block of limestone, now in Oxford.

(This was erected) in the 2nd year of Servius Galba, Emperor Caesar Augustus, on the 21st of the month Neosebastos (November).

Galba began his reign on June 9th, 68 A.D. Therefore he would enter on a second year, according to Egyptian reckoning, on August 29th following (= 1st of Thoth). The month Neosebastos is the equivalent of Athyr (= October—November), and occurs often enough in papyri (*v.* Führer durch die Ausstellung d. pap. Rainer, p. 66, etc.); but, so far as I know, it has not been found before in an inscription.

No. III.

Imp(erator) Caesar Domitianus Aug(ustus)
Germanicus Pontif(ex) Maximus trib(uniciae)
potest(atis) consul XV censor perpetuus p(ater)
 p(atriae)
    pontem a solo fecit.
[. . . . .]
Q. Licinnio Ancotio Proculo praef(ecto)
 castr(orum),
L. Antistio Asiatico praef(ecto) Beren(ices),
cura C. Iuli Magni (centurionis) leg(ionis) III
 Cyr(enaicae).

47. On a slab of limestone, bought at Coptos, now in the British Museum.

The Emperor Caesar Domitian Augustus Germanicus, supreme pontiff, invested with tribunician power, consul for the 15th time, perpetual censor, father of his country, built up the bridge from its foundations.

. . . . being governor of Egypt; Quintus Licinnius Ancotius Proculus being prefect of the camps; Lucius Antistius Asiaticus being prefect of the Red Sea slope. The erection was supervised by Caius Julius Magnus, centurion of the Third Cyrenaic Legion.

(This will appear in C. I. L. III. Suppl. 3, No. 13,580.)

The number of the consulship fixes this to the year 90 A.D. The bridge in question must have been thrown over the large irrigation canal which, we may be sure, passed just west of Coptos in Roman times, as it passes now.

The name erased is that of the Eparch of Egypt. We know from published sources four Eparchs in the reign of Domitian :—

C. Laelius Africanus,   in office in 82 A.D.
C. Septimius Vegetus   „   „ 86 „
T. Petronius Secundus „   „ 95 „
Mettius Rufus   „   „ ?

It is possible that the fourth of these names is the one to be supplied in this and in the Tariff inscription (*infra*, No. IV). The Eparchs held office generally for three years at least, and it will be noticed that the three officers whose periods are known, leave a gap about the year 90. Furthermore, the manner in which Suetonius (Vit. Dom. 4) introduces the name of Mettius Rufus suggests that there was something unsatisfactory, which laid the nomination of that officer open to canvass. If he were a disreputable individual, or a creature of the Emperor, a reason would be supplied for the erasure of his name here. His master's name has been hacked out with his on the Tariff *stela*. In any case the erased name can hardly be that of any of the first three Eparchs in the list above, for all are found elsewhere unmutilated in inscriptions of Egypt. The erasure here conceals either the name of Mettius Rufus or of an unknown Eparch.

The *praefectus castrorum* is the regular title of a legionary commander in Egypt. He was of equestrian, not senatorial, rank, like the *legati* commanding legions elsewhere ; and this distinction was due to Augustus' special organisation of Egypt on Ptolemaic lines as a sort of vast royal domain, to the exclusion of all officials of senatorial dignity. (Tac. Ann. ii. 59. Hist. i. 11. Arrian, Anab. Al. 3, 5.) Q. Licinnius Ancotius Proculus is not known otherwise. He commanded, of course, Legio III Cyrenaica, whose headquarters were probably at Coptos, but whose component parts were distributed widely.

The individual, who is prefect of the eastern slopes and Red Sea ports, is mentioned in the Tariff below, but not elsewhere. A family of Antistii, springing from Thibilis in Numidia, produced persons of official rank in the 1st and 3rd centuries, and probably this individual is of their stock. (C. I. L. VIII. Suppl. 18893–18906 : C. I. Rh. 55.)

No. IV.

'Εξ ἐπιταγῆς . . . .
. . . . "Οσα δεῖ τοὺς μισθω-
τὰς τοῦ ἐν Κόπτῳ ὑποπείπτον-

τος τῇ 'Αραβαρχίᾳ ἀποστολίου πράσ-
σειν κατὰ τ(ὸ)ν γνώμονα τῇδε τῇ   5
στήλη ἐνκεχάρακται διὰ Λουκίου
'Αντιστίου 'Ασιατικοῦ ἐπάρχου
"Ορους Βερενείκης.
Κυβερνήτου ἐρυθραικοῦ δρα-
χμὰς ὀκτώ.   10
Πρωρέως δραχμὰς δέκα.
. . . . ακου δραχμὰς δέκα.
Να]ύτου δραχμὰς πέντε.
Θεραπ]εύτου ναυπηγοῦ δραχμὰς
πέντε. Χειροτέχνου δραχμὰς   15
ὀκτώ. Γυναικῶν πρὸς ἑταιρισ-
μὸν δραχμὰς ἕκατον ὀκτώ.
Γυναικῶν εἰσπλεουσῶν δρα-
χμὰς εἴκοσι. Γυναικῶν στρατι-
ωτῶν δραχμὰς εἴκοσι.   20
Πιττακίου καμήλων ὀβολὸν ἔνα.
Σφραγισμοῦ πιττακίου ὀβολοὺς δύο.
Πορείας ἐξερχομένης ἐκάστου
πιττακίου τοῦ ἀνδρὸς ἀναβαίνον-
τος δραχμὴν μίαν. Γυναικῶν   25
πασῶν ἀνὰ δραχμὰς τέσσαρας.
"Ονου ὀβολοὺς δύο. 'Αμάξης ἐχού-
σης τετράγωνον δραχμὰς τέσσαρες.
'Ιστοῦ δραχμὰς εἴκοσι. Κέρατος δραχμὰς τέσσαρες. Ταφῆς ἀναφερομέ-   30
νης καὶ καταφερομένης δραχμὴν μ[ί-
αν τετρώβολον. ('Ετους) θ' Αὐτοκράτορος
Καίσαρος [Δομιτιανοῦ] Σεβαστοῦ [Γερμαν(ικοῦ)]
παχὼ ιε'.

48. On a tablet of nummulitic limestone in the Ghizeh Museum ; found halfway between Coptos and the desert at the remains of a guard-house (?) on the road across the plain.

By order of [. . . *governor of Egypt.*] *The dues, which the lessees of the transport service in Coptos, subject to the Arabian command, are authorized to levy by the customary scale, are inscribed on this slab at the instance of L. Antistius Asiaticus, prefect of the Red Sea slope.*

For a Red Sea helmsman . .	*drachmas*	8.	—
„ „ „ *bowsman* . .	„	10.	—
„ *?*	„	10.	—
„ *an able seaman* . . .	„	5.	—
„ *a shipyard hand* . . .	„	5.	—
„ *a skilled artisan* . . .	„	8.	—
„ *women for prostitution* .	„	108.	—
„ *women, immigrant* . .	„	20.	—

For wives of soldiers . . . drachmas 20. —
„ *a camel-ticket* . . . . — — obol 1.
„ *sealing of said ticket* . . — — „ 2.
„ *each ticket for the husband,*
if mounted, when a cara-
van is leaving the city . „ 1 —
„ *all his women at the rate of* „ 4 —
„ *an ass* . . . . . . — — „ 2.
„ *a waggon with tilt* . . „ 4 —
„ *a ship's mast* . . . . „ 20. —
„ „ *yard* . . . . „ 4. —
„ *a funeral up to the desert*
and back. . . . . „ 1 „ 4

The 9th year of the Emperor Caesar (Domitian)
Augustus (Germanicus) on the 15th of the month
Pachon (May).

This falls in May, 90 A.D., since Domitian began
his reign in September, almost at the beginning of
the Egyptian year.

49. l. 1. The erased name is no doubt the same as
that obliterated in No. III, *supra*, dated in the same
year, 90 A.D.

l. 2. Μισθωτής, "one who pays rent," in this case to
the Emperor. The term is more particularly appro-
priate to farmers of dues accruing directly to the
Emperor, as did those of Egypt, which the Romans
took from the Ptolemies and continued to regard as a
single Royal Estate. This abnormal condition of
Egypt accounts probably, as we shall see below, for
the unusual character of this Tariff. Egypt was full
of such μισθωταί, farming mines (*e.g.*, in *Jebel Fatireh*,
C. I. G. 4713 f.), dues on mining or customs at
Syene (μ. ἱερᾶς πύλης Σοήνης, C. I. G. 4867,
4868, etc., etc.), customs, rents of estates, etc., in the
Oases. See also the very interesting inscription of
Khargeh (C. I. G. 4957), a decree of the Jewish
Eparch, Ti. Jul. Alexander, in the reign of Galba,
that no one thenceforward might be coerced to take up
a μίσθωσις. This latter decree shows that, since Nero
had reformed the abuses of the publicanus system by
insisting on the publication of tariffs (Tac. Ann. xiii.
50, 51), the farming of dues had ceased to provoke
competition; and the Imperial administration had
been forced to resort to compulson to keep the cheap
and convenient system of private collection of dues in
general operation at all.

l. 4. The Ἀραβάρχης, an official taken over by the
Romans from the Ptolemies, held command over the
eastern desert up to the Red Sea, and had therefore

the chief control of caravan trade, and the collection
of customs at Red Sea ports. Sometimes his office
was combined with the *Epistrategia* of the Thebaid
(cf. C. I. G. 4751), and he was styled, *e.g.*, στρατηγὸς
τῆς Ἰνδικῆς καὶ Ἐρυθρᾶς θαλάσσης (C. I. G. 4897 b)—
but at the period of this inscription the Ἀραβαρχία
evidently was controlled by the Prefect of Mons
Berenice, whose peculiar sphere of jurisdiction was the
Red Sea littoral. Coptos itself, however, was in the
Epistrategia of the Thebaid, and the Prefect of
Mons Berenice exercises authority in this city only in
its relation to the great desert roads which it was his
peculiar province to maintain and defend.

l. 4. Ἀποστόλιον, a word otherwise unknown. Its
sense must depend, therefore, on the general interpretation of the character of this Tariff, *v. infra*.

l. 6. *L. Antistius Asiaticus*, v. *supra* on No. III.

l. 8. *Mons Berenices* = the eastern slope of the Arabian
chain, which rises steeply from the Red Sea. Its re-
moteness and inaccessibility rendered it necessary, in
any period not wholly peaceful, that a special governor
should be appointed, v. note *supra* on Ἀραβάρχης.

l. 10. There are traces of a thorough erasure under
this line, and at the beginning of l. 11. Two letters
survive faintly, shewing that something had been
assessed at 6 drachmas.

l. 12. I can suggest no satisfactory restoration.
No ship's officer or hand is designated by a word
ending in -ακος. It is just possible that the word is
Νειλι]ακοῦ, but there seems hardly sufficient room for
so many letters, and it is hard to see for what a Nile
boatman would cross the desert, nor why he is distinguished from the other general classes of seamen.

ll. 13, 14. Restoration practically certain.

l. 21. Πιττάκιον, originally the sealing of a jar, is
used here in the derived sense of a *label* or *ticket*
(cf. Brit. Mus. Pap. 121, l. 412). The traveller did not
pay on the several beasts, but on the ticket, which
presumably gave him the right to hire camels for the
road or to use them upon it. He pays both on
receiving the said ticket and on having it stamped.
I know no parallels to these items. It was a general
principle of Roman rating not to tax beasts (cf. Tariff
of Zarai, C. I. L. viii. No. 4508, *pecora in nundinium*
immunia and a well-known Decree of Constantine
the Great), but rather their burdens only. Nevertheless we find at Palmyra that on the camel itself a
denarius has to be paid both going and coming, and
whether loaded or not. The Palmyrene Tariff, how-

ever, is that of a local *octroi* (v. Cagnat *cit. infra*), not of the Imperial *Portorium*.

ll. 23, 24. Σφραγισμός is not found in this sense in classical Greek; but the context is sufficient to establish the interpretation.

l. 28. The waggon intended is evidently one for the conveyance of passengers, and furnished with a tilt. Such a vehicle could have passed easily over the Roman road through the Wady Hammamat. This Tariff seems to have no reference to merchandise.

l. 30. Compare a provision in the Digest (xi. 7, 37). "*Funeris sumptus accipitur quidquid corporis causa . . . erogatum est . . . vel si qua vectigalia sunt, vel sarcophagi vel vectura.*" Justinian suppressed the taxing of funerals (Cod. III, 44, 15) "*in nullo quopiam loco vectigal ab aliqua persona pro corporibus, ex uno in alium locum translatis, praestetur.*"

The ἀνα- and κατα- in this case must signify *up* to the cemetery in the Desert (which lies of course higher than the cultivated land about the city, and is always called in Egypt *el gebel*, "the mountain"); and returning *down* to the town. The same particles usually imply in Egypt a course up or down stream on the Nile (cf. Strabo, p. 800, in connection with boats paying dues at Schedia); but this inscription applies obviously not to the river, but to the desert road.

The word ταφή is used in the late cemeteries of Thebes, as though equivalent to τάφος, and probably it means generally an "interment," rather than a coffin (which would not *return* from the desert) or a bier.

l. 33. The comparison of No. III makes the restoration of the Emperor's name certain. The letters are much crowded in the last line, but still there is not room for more than an abbreviated form of *Germanicus*, or, possibly, for *Germ. Dac.*

50. On the occasion of the levying by Caligula in Rome of certain novel imposts, the most part in themselves not objectionable, the people, as Suetonius tells us (Cal. 41), finding that much friction resulted from ignorance of the exact dues, prayed the Emperor to publish the new Tariff. The eccentric ruler of the world accordingly had an inscription engraved in microscopic lettering and set it up in a place so remote and inaccessible, that no one was a jot the wiser.

The evil complained of then was not confined to Rome. The exactions which have made the word *publicanus* a term of reproach, were aggravated all over the Empire by the absence of precise statements as to the amounts which could be levied legally; and at last Nero, checked by the Senate in a quixotic design to abolish tax-farming at one stroke, promulgated a decree that all dues exacted by *publicani* according to vague local custom, or private rule, should be reduced to writing and set up for all the world to read (Tac. Ann. xiii. 50, 51). In the province of customs, *octroi*-dues and the like, (to which we must confine ourselves now) this wise decree would entail the publication only of the rates on such items as were not saleable commodities in the ordinary sense, for the duty on these latter was *ad valorem*, at a rate fixed generally but variously for different provinces (cf. R. Cagnat, *Les impôts indirects chez les romains*, pp. 13 ff.), and proclaimed by the local τελωνικὸς νόμος.

None of the Tariffs set up at Nero's instance have survived to our day; indeed we do not know whether action followed on his decree or not. In the succeeding century and a half, however, we find three inscriptions, the motive for whose erection is most probably the same as that which prompted his policy. The earliest is the one which I publish here, set up at Coptos in the year 90, in the reign of Domitian. The next was engraved at Palmyra in 136, under Hadrian; and the third at Zarai in Numidia in 202, during the joint reign of Septimius Severus and his eldest son. (The Palmyrene text is published best by De Vogué in *Journ. Asiat.* 1883, ii. p. 149; less completely by Foucart in *Bull. de corresp. hellénique*, 1882, vi. pp. 439 ff. Commented on by R. Cagnat in *Rev. de Phil.* 1884, pp. 135 ff.; and by H. Dessau in *Hermes*, xix. pp. 486 ff. I have used frequently, in what follows, the comments of both the last-named authorities. The Numidian text is in C. I. L. viii. 4508. The stone is in the Louvre.)

The three inscriptions differ widely in character. That at Palmyra is an *octroi*-tariff in Greek and Aramaic applying to the city and its immediate territory, and set up, as its Preamble declares, to put an end to frequent disputes between collectors and merchants. (Cf. same motive for the publication in Justinian's time of the dues to be levied in the Dardanelles, Mordtmann in *Mittheil. d. deutsch. arch. Inst. in Athen*, iv. p. 308.) There had existed previously in Palmyra a general τελωνικὸς νόμος; but the dues on only very few articles were stated particularly, it being written in general terms in the lease granted to the farmer, that he should levy rates ἀκολούθως τῷ νόμῳ καὶ τῇ συνηθείᾳ. Palmyra had been included but very recently in the Roman Empire, and had applied already, as this law shews, before its incorporation to Roman governors (*e.g.* Corbulo in Nero's reign) for rulings on points in dispute with regard to customs-dues.

The *Tariff of Zarai*, on the other hand, refers to the *douane* at the port ; and was set up *post discessum cohortis*, which fact implies, in the opinion of M. Cagnat (*Les impôts, cit. supra*, p. 116), that so long as a garrison had remained in the town, there had been no *douane*, soldiers being free from all such dues (*Tac. Ann.* l.c.). This Tariff takes account only of a small number of items, and those such as might be supposed, reasonably, not to be determined by the general Regulation of the *Portorium* for the province of Numidia. It is in fact a local supplement to the general Tariff of the province.

This *Tariff of Coptos* is wholly distinct from either of the other two ; and can be compared with them only so far as the motive of its erection is concerned. Unfortunately for the commentator, it is unique in almost every respect ; there exists no parallel to it as a whole in any part of the Roman world, nor has it instructive points of contact in detail with the facts of the financial organisation of the Empire as known to us. It owes this singularity, no doubt, to the unique constitution of Egypt, inherited by the Emperors from the Ptolemies as a sort of private royal estate (cf. Mommsen, Hist. vol. v., Eng. tr. vol. 2, c. 12), and never organised or administered like any other province, senatorial or imperial. In determining therefore the nature of this Tariff, we must work mainly from its own internal evidence.

The first and greatest difficulty arises from the fact that the word ἀποστόλιον (l. 4), which describes the nature of the whole Tariff, is not found elsewhere. Its etymology suggests that it has reference to an ἀπόστολος, something despatched. Let us see if an examination of other points in the inscription will enable us to assign a more precise meaning.

51. This Tariff is set up at the immediate instance, not of the *epistrategos* of the Thebaid, in whose jurisdiction Coptos itself lay, but of the Prefect of the Red Sea slope. It cannot, therefore, be a local *octroi* of Coptos, but must relate to something outside the territory of that town, and lying within the Arabarchia. The dues called ἀποστόλιον, whatever they may be, are collected for convenience only in Coptos, but are controlled by and paid over to the Arabarch.

Might it not be, however, like the Tariff of Zarai, a supplement to the General Regulation of the Imperial *Portorium?* Be it noted, however, that, unlike the Zarai Tariff, this list at Coptos does not concern itself with commodities. Except the mast and yard (l. 29), and the prostitutes (l. 16), none of its *items* could be called *res venales*. Furthermore, if it be a Tariff of the Portorium of the Red Sea (for the *douanes* on the littoral, see Peripl. Mar. Erythr. p. 11 ; Strabo, xvii. p. 798), why are not the dues mentioned in it collected, together with those on ordinary commodities, at the Red Sea ports? Nor can it well be referred to a *second Portorium* paid on entrance to the Nile valley ; for what would the Prefect of Mons Berenice have to do with that? and how could the merchandise, landed on the bare shores of Berenice or Myos Hormos for the sole purpose of being conveyed to Egypt, be expected to pay twice over, before ever attaining Egypt at all? Had such a system been in force, there would have been but little trade on the Berenice-Coptos road.

The Arabarch was concerned simply with the Red Sea ports and the roads leading thence to the Nile valley. If this Tariff has not to do with the ports, it must have to do with the roads. If we look down the list of items, we note that, with the exception of the mast and yard, it refers entirely to persons, beasts for transit, vehicles for transit, and funerals, going up to and returning from the desert—in short, to traffic on a road.

These facts being taken together with the etymological meaning of the word, the conclusion suggests itself that ἀποστόλιον must mean something like a *posting service*, the despatch of caravans from point to point under the protection of the imperial government, and on a road made, maintained, and controlled directly by the Arabarch. For the use of this road, and for escort thereon, certain dues are charged according to a scale (γνώμων) already existent by custom, but now published for the first time: and the collection of these dues is farmed out to lessees, and made for convenience at Coptos rather than at the ports.

The absence, however, of dues on merchandise, the transport of which must have constituted the main part of the traffic on the road, calls for some explanation. I will suggest two possible reasons for the omission, and of the two I prefer the second : First, that, since commodities would be taxed in any case at the port on entering or leaving, the claim of the ἀποστόλιον may have been satisfied out of the *portorium*. Secondly, that commodities paid an *ad valorem* duty, which (as in the case of the *portorium* dues), did not admit of being stated in a Tariff, since the amounts levied would vary infinitely. The existing γνώμων settled the percentage, and that general rate was already known to all the world.

The items in this Tariff are such as cannot be rated *ad valorem*, and the statement of them is, in fact, like the Tariff at Zarai, supplementary to an existing Regulation. It is not easy to determine whether the payments are made on arriving at Coptos from the Red Sea, or on leaving Coptos for the Red Sea: it seems that the dues in this Tariff refer to journeys in both directions. I would suggest that up to l. 20 the items due are to be paid on arrival at Coptos : from l. 20 to l. 30 they are to be paid in advance before departure. Lines 30–32 refer to a local use of the road as an approach to the cemeteries in the eastern desert.

To justify this distinction let us look at the items. The first group might be interpreted equally, as arrivals or departures, were it not that, whereas there is no obvious reason why mariners and craftsmen should come from the littoral into the Nile valley, which abounded in such already, there is every reason why they should go down to the desolate and thinly-populated littoral of the Red Sea. There must always have been a demand for fresh hands to man the merchant fleets, far beyond what barren settlements, like Berenice or Myos Hormos, dependent, as Kosseir is nowadays, on cistern-water, could supply. Ἐρυθραικοῦ, therefore, will mean "*for* the Red Sea."

The second group, the women, could hardly be anything but arrivals, even did not the word εἰσπλεουσῶν occur. Prostitutes, paying at the huge rate of 108 drachmas, could ply their trade at a profit only in the greatest cities of the empire : and there were but few soldiers, beyond auxiliary bowmen (Pliny, N. H. vi. 101), exiled to Berenice.

52. The enormous duty here levied on prostitutes needs some explanation. We know already that πορνόβοσκοι paid on their women at the frontiers of the Empire. In Philostratus' life of Apollonius of Tyana (i. 18 qu. by Dessau in Hermes, xix. pp. 486, *seq.*), it is told how that holy man was stopped by a collector at the crossing of Euphrates, and asked his wares. He replied that he brought with him Σωφροσύνη, Δικαιοσύνη, Ἀνδρεία and the like. The collector was about to assess these as δούλας, but was assured hastily by the prophet that he had meant, not δούλας, but δεσποίνας. But, so far as I am aware, the scale of dues is not

known elsewhere than here at Coptos. Inside the Empire prostitutes were taxed individually, *e.g.*, at Rome, under Caligula (Suet. Cal. 40), *quantum quaeque uno concubitu mereret*, and the Emperor decreed further *ut tenerentur publico et quae meretricium quivi lenocinium fecissent*. The Tariff of Palmyra also prescribes that such women shall pay at the rate of a single fee, if that be a *denarius* or more. (See R. Cagnat, in *Rev. de Phil.* 1884, pp. 135, ff.).

The *graffiti* of Pompeii reveal to us that the vulgar fee was a denarius per act. How, then, could the purveyors afford to pay 108 drachmas on imported women? Two explanations are possible : (1) That the rate at Coptos is intended to be prohibitive, in order that a certain class of Eastern prostitute should not be imported in great numbers to corrupt health and manners : perhaps Coptos with its large garrison needed especial protection ; (2) That some peculiarly fashionable class of prostitute was imported from the Red Sea. I know no positive evidence for this last fact, but prefer to conjecture that such was the case, rather than import Protection into this Tariff. It would certainly not be to the obvious interest of the government or lessees to discourage the use of the Coptos-Berenice road, and it is easier to suppose that a high rate was exacted because it would be paid, than that it was demanded in order to prohibit (cf. Cagnat, *Impôts*, etc. *cit. supra*, p. 3). We have to do in this clause not with women for private concubinage, but those for the supply of public brothels, and must infer that in the great cities (as distinguished from such little towns as Pompeii) there was a demand for Arabian, Indian or negro women, which admitted of very high fees being asked for and paid.

The "*women, immigrant*," are probably those coming voluntarily, and not under the charge of a πορνόβοσκος. Such would become harlots, living apart, or private concubines.

The item "*wives of soldiers*" recalls the fact that in Domitian's time the legionaries everywhere contracted unrecognised marriages and begot children, who remained *sine civitate*, unless legitimized on the occasion of their father's *missio honesta* (see Mommsen in C. I. L. iii. p. 905 ; and M. and Marquardt, fr. tr. xi. p. 307). In fact, before the time of Severus, *justum matrimonium* was not possible for a legionary while serving with the colours. But in Egypt the illegitimate children of such were enrolled not infrequently as legionaries, even as early as the first century, before they had received *civitas :* and Mommsen (Eph. Epigr. v. p. 12) remarks on this fact as proof of the rule of the Emperors having been laxer in Egypt than elsewhere. The provision in our Tariff agrees in shewing some kind of recognition of the illegitimate unions of soldiers.

At line 21 we seem to begin the Tariff of departures. The ticket for camels must surely be paid for in advance, and presently, in l. 23, the word ἐξερχομένης removes all doubt.

Lines 24–28 seem undoubtedly to refer to family migrations. The head of the family, distinguished by the definite article, pays one drachma, being a passenger, and rich enough not to go on foot: his women (wives and slaves together), who would be mounted on camels in any case, and often two on a camel, pay four drachmas the lot. If, however, women or others use single asses, they pay two obols, and if the more luxurious waggon is requisitioned (the eastern *araba* of the present day), then they pay four drachmas. This refers probably to native polygamous races, such as the Bedawin nowadays.

The mast and yard are taxed perhaps because it was the custom (as it is still) to convey long timbers from place to place, half hitched up on a camel, half dragging behind: and accordingly a rather heavy charge is made to compensate for the wear and tear of the roadway. But if the yards and masts were at all of the dimensions of those of modern *dahabiyahs*, they would have to be dragged altogether, or carried slung to several camels at once: in either case a heavy charge would be still more reasonable.

The fact that these articles are mentioned at all shews that there must have been a considerable transport of *northern* straight poles up the Nile and across the desert to supply the eastern fleets.

53. The semi-official transport service, which this Tariff seems to imply, is singular in the Imperial organisation, and must be due to the special difficulties and dangers of the Red Sea routes—difficulties and dangers which the appointment of a district prefect to command the littoral implies in any case (Cf. Mommsen, Prov., Eng. tr. c. 12). Such a service bears no relation to any of the facts known about the Imperial Post (*cursus publicus* or *fiscalis*), which, as a source of expense to the subjects of the Empire, and later in part to the Treasury, not of profit (cf. excellent art. in Daremberg and Saglio, Dict. Ant. s. v. *Cursus*), cannot be conceived as leased to μισθωταί. Moreover the Post, existing as it did only for the transport of government messages and material, and for occasional use by those favoured

with a special *diploma* from the Emperor or (at times) his Pretorian prefect or *magister officiorum*, could have no concern with many of the items in this Tariff. The first group of items might conceivably be connected with the *naves publicae*, but why should they pay to μισθωταί, and what about the other groups?

The identity of the road in question here is beyond doubt. It is that great highway, which forked shortly after leaving Coptos, northwards to Myos Hormos, southwards to Berenice. Both branches are described by Strabo (pp. 814–816) and by Pliny (N. H. vi. 102, cf. 23 & v. 2, 60; Xen. Eph. iv. 2), as supplied with cisterns and *khans*, the maintenance of which would entail, on so desert a track, much trouble and expense. In a Latin inscription found some years ago at Coptos (C. I. L. iii. suppl. 6627), we have an interesting record of the labour expended by detachments of the troops stationed in Egypt on the repair of the cisterns and roadway on the Myos Hormos and the Berenice routes. As to the need for protection, that may safely be taken for granted; the Romans never crushed the Bedawin of the north any more than the Axomites of the south, or the pirates who infested the Red Sea, and rendered constant patrolling imperative (Pliny, N. H. vi. 101).

The importance of these caravan routes in the time of Domitian was enormous; and most important was the road from Berenice, which, though longer, started from a more convenient port than Myos Hormos. The other well-known route from Berenice to the Nile opposite Hermopolis Parva, was not opened out by Hadrian until 137 A.D. (See inscription of Antinoe, found at Sheikh Abadeh, and qu. by Lumbroso, *Egitto al tempo dei greci e dei romani*, c. iv.) The more southern route from Leuce Come to Syene (Assuân) was not nearly so much in favour as those to Coptos, partly owing to the great distance of desert to be traversed, partly also, it seems, owing to definite discouragement by the Romans. Only on such a supposition can the enormous rate of 25 per cent., levied both on imports and exports at Leuce Come (Peripl. l. c. cf. Strabo, xvii. p. 798), be accounted for. Such figures only become intelligible if the Imperial Government, which had been at great expense and trouble to make, maintain, and protect the Coptos routes, had to depend for reimbursement on the caravan tax with which our inscription is concerned. It might in that case determine very reasonably to confine trade to these latter routes.

Its policy, however, was not wholly successful, as the existence of a great mart at Syene for spices, gems, and Indian and Arabian products generally sufficiently proves; but nevertheless a vast proportion (cf. Arist. Or. 48, p. 485) of the commerce with Arabia, India, and the still farther East, arrived at or started from Coptos, and gave to that place a fame as the trading-town *par excellence* of inland Egypt, which devolved after the Arab conquest on the neighbouring Kous, served by the same roads, and by the port of Aïdab. (See on this slight geographical change, Heyd, *Commerce du Levant*, vol. i. c. 8, pp. 380 ff.). And a shadow of the same repute lingers still with Keneh, lying a little north of Kuft (Coptos), and equally at the outlet of the old Coptos caravan route. But it is the shadow of a shade. The discovery of a sea-way round the Cape dealt the first blow; the opening of the overland route to Suez the second; the cutting of the canal the last and deadliest; and even the construction of the projected railway from Keneh to Koseir will not revive all the glories of the great desert route to the East.

No. V.

Εὐσεβ(ε)ία[ς χ]άριν ἐ[π' ἀγα-
θῷ · (ἔτους) ιε' Λουκίου
Σεπτιμίου Σεουή[ρου
Εὐσεβοῦς Περτίνακ[ος
καὶ Μάρκου Αὐρηλίου
'Αντωνίνου Εὐσεβοῦς
Σεβαστῶν φαρμ[ουθὶ

. . . .

54. On a piece of a small column of sandstone, now at Oxford.

In token of piety and for good fortune (this was erected) in the 15th year of Lucius Septimius Severus Pius Pertinax, and of Marcus Aurelius Antoninus Pius, joint Augusti on the ..th of the month Pharmouthi (April).

As Severus began his reign in June, this falls in April, 207 A.D. In Egypt the son, Caracalla, is regarded habitually as having reigned with his father since 193, not as from his formal association in 198. Cf. *infra*, No. VI.

No. VI.

"Ετους κδ'
τοῦ κυρίου
ἡμῶν αὐτοκράτορο[ς
Σεουήρου 'Αντωνίνου
Εὐσεβοῦς Εὐτυχοῦς

Σεβαστοῦ ἐπεὶφ κ'.
Θεῷ μεγίστῳ 'Ιεραβ-
λῳ Μ. Αὐρήλιος
Βηλάκαβος 'Ιερα(πολίτης ?)
οὐηξιλλάριος
'Αδριανῶν Παλμ[υ-
ρηνῶν 'Αντωνινιανῶν
τοξότων.

55. On an altar of limestone bought at Coptos, now in University College.

In the 24th year of our Lord Emperor Severus Antoninus Pius Felix Augustus, on the 20th of the month Epiphi (July), to the most high god, Hierablous, Marcus Aurelius Belakabos of Hierapolis?, vexillarius of Hadrian's Antoninian Palmyrene Archers, (erected this).

This falls in July, 216 A.D., the year before Caracalla's murder. Cf. the note on the preceding inscription.

l. 7. The name of the god, identical with the place-name *Jerablûs* in Syria, is most interesting. It is highly probable that he is the god of that city, bearing its original name, rationalized later by the Greeks in the familiar form *Hierapolis*. Instances of such rationalization, and of subsequent reversion to the original form, occur all over the East; the best example is Jerusalem—Hierosolyma. As a god's name, Hierablous occurs here only. He has been imported of course by the Syrian archers.

l. 9. The name Βηλάκαβος occurs also in an inscription of Palmyra (C. I. G. 4495). It = Baal-Yakub and has been found on an early scarab of a Syrian invader of Egypt (IXth dynasty?) named Yakub-hal or -el; and in the place-names of the list of Palestine towns conquered by Thothmes III (XVIIIth dynasty) occurs *Yakeb-el*.

The ethnic 'Ιερα(πολίτης) cannot be regarded as certain, the right edge of the stone being much worn; but it is certain that there is room only for a contracted word. Such a word would be almost sure to be an ethnic, and in that case can hardly be other than 'Ιεραπολίτης.

l. 10. A *vexillarius* of an auxiliary corps is unusual, but not without precedent. Cf. *e.g.* C. I. L. iii. 4576, 4834, 2012, 2744.

This corps of archers (not mentioned elsewhere, so far as I am aware), appropriately takes its first title from the Emperor who incorporated Palmyra in the Empire. In connection with its presence at Coptos it is worth while to recall the fact that fifty years later than the period of this inscription, Coptos was the chief stronghold of the Palmyrene party in Egypt. There the Blemmyes (Vopiscus, Aurel. p. 239, D. ed. Salmasius), called to her aid by Zenobia, remained in possession until the reign of Probus, and thither, no doubt, the broken remnants of Firmus' insurgents retired from Aurelian. ("*Idem et cum Blemmyis societatem maximam tenuit.*" "*Hic ergo contra Aurelianum sumpsit imperium ad defendendas partes quae supererant Zenobiae.*" Vopisc., Vita Firmi, p. 243, ff.) How did the Palmyrene archers in garrison receive Firmus and the Blemmyes? It is much more probable that they were for Odenathus and Zenobia than for Gallienus and Aurelian. Unfortunately we know no facts as to the attitude of the auxiliaries in Egypt at this crisis. We know only from the *Notitia Dignitatum* that at the end of the next century no Palmyrene archers were in garrison at Coptos, their place having been taken by native Egyptian levies. In fact no Palmyrene corps of archers is mentioned in the *Notitia* at all, or in any other authority. We may infer therefore, with some assurance, that the Coptos corps was soon disbanded, and suggest that the cause of its disbandment was connected with the Palmyrene insurrection.

No. VII.

Ὑπὲρ διαμονῆς [. . . . . . .
Κυιητοῦ Σεβασ[τοῦ . . . καὶ τοῖς συννάοις
θεοῖς τὸ τέμε[νος . . . .
αυτο ἀνδριὰς [. . . . . . .
Ἄρειος ὁ καὶ Σ[. . . . . . .
βουλευτὴς [. . . . . . .
ἐρ]υθραικὸς συ[. . . . . . .

56. On a slab of variegated marble, bought at Coptos; now in University College.

This stone represents only a small fragment of the surface originally inscribed. In the latter portion of l. 1, for instance, we should expect the name of Macrianus and the praenomen and nomen (Caius Fulvius) of Quietus, and his titles. A god and his titles have disappeared from l. 2. Where so much is lost, it is idle to attempt restoration.

This inscription is of great interest, being, so far as I can discover, one of only two epigraphic memorials of the usurpation of Quietus in the East. The other, to which Prof. W. M. Ramsay called my attention, was found at Nacoleia. It is dedicated, he says, to τὸν γῆς καὶ θαλάσσης δεσπότην Γ. φουλούιον Ἰούνιον Κυαιτὸν. Mordtmann, I believe, published it in Münch. Sitz. 1862. I cannot verify the reference, that periodical not being in the Bodleian. There are coins and also papyri (1) dated in 1st year of Macrianus and Quietus (Mittheil. aus d. Samml. d. pap. Rainer, 2 and 3, pp. 28–33); (2) No. 50 in *Alexandrian Erotic fragm.*, etc., by B. P. Grenfell, Clar. Press, Oxford. Quietus, son of Macrianus, assumed the purple in 259 A.D., together with his father and brother, while the Empire lay distracted after the defeat and capture of Valerian. While his co-usurpers marched on Rome, Quietus turned to Egypt, but did not stay long, for the family venture soon proved a failure, and a stronger usurper than he, the Palmyrene Odenathus, husband of the famous Zenobia, took the field against him. Quietus returned to Syria, and was slain at Emesa in 261 or early in 262. This inscription falls therefore, in all likelihood, in 260.

This is all that we know of Quietus' history, gathered from Trebellius Pollio's jejune sketches of him and of Odenathus (XXX Tyrann.). This inscription has therefore unusual interest, both as confirming the fact of Quietus' expedition to Egypt, and tending to shew that he was more successful there than the historian states. He must have begun in Egypt, indeed, that period of detachment from the central rule, which continued until the time of Probus. Odenathus only crushed Quietus in order himself to rule the East, and after his death Firmus raised Egypt again in the Palmyrene interest against Aurelian; and, although the latter was victorious, we know that Coptos and Upper Egypt remained in the hands of the Blemmyes, allies of the Palmyrenes, invited from Nubia in the first instance by Zenobia. Coptos was in fact a centre of revolt from the date of the erection of this inscription until the expedition of Probus. Cf. *supra*, No. VI.

No. VIII.

Θε[ᾷ μεγ]ίστῃ
Ἴσιδι ὑπὲρ
εὐπλοίας
πλοίου Σαρά-
πιδος Ἑρμα[ιος. ?

57. On a small column of limestone, now in University College.

To the most high goddess, Isis, for a fair voyage for the ship, Serapis, Hermaeus ? (dedicates this).

A propitiatory offering by a merchant or shipowner engaged in the Red Sea trade.

No. IX.

Πουὼν ϛ' Ἁρπάη-
σις ἀνέθηκεν τῷ
ἰδίῳ θεῷ μεγίστῳ.

On a block of limestone now at Manchester.

On the 6th of the month Pauni (= June), Arpaesis erected (this) to his own most high god.

The month is misspelt, and the form of *stigma* is unusual (although easily to be derived from the normal form), but there can be no doubt as to the interpretation.

The name Arpaesis occurs at Silseleh (C. I. G. 4847) and at Philae (C. I. G. 4915, b.).

What god is intended by this mysterious formula was left doubtful, perhaps with intention, by the dedicator. Serapis or Pan-Khem are the most likely to be termed μέγιστος: but the studied obscurity in this case raises a faint suspicion that the dedication may be to the God of the Christians. I know no parallel to this formula.

No. X.

Ἀριστόνεικος Διδύ[μου
ἀδελφὸς ἐρῶν
πτα
Εὐψύχει.

On a stele of nummulitic limestone in Egyptian style, representing the mummified deceased introduced by Anubis before Osiris and Isis.

No. XI.

. . λαβδῷ ? Ἀπό[λλωνι
. Μ. Αὐρήλιος Σε[. . . . ?
νις β' τὸν νάον οἰκ[οδόμησεν,
ἐξωγράφησεν τὴ[ν . . . .
θιν, ἐποίησεν ἐκ τοῦ [ἰδίου κόπου
τὸ προσκύνημα.
ἐπ' ἀγαθ[ῷ.

P. 18. I may add to the propylon inscriptions named on p. 18 at Coptos and Dendera, two others just discovered at Kom Ushim = Karanis, in the Fayum, under a late (unknown) Ptolemy, and also under Commodus. See the forthcoming number of the E. E. F. Arch. Report.

P. 23. I had intended to republish the Victorinus inscription given on p. 23, but it is not to be found in the Ghizeh Museum ; and I have since heard that it has not gone further than Keneh.

INDEX.

G

LONDON : PRINTED BY WILLIAM CLOWES AND SONS, LIMITED, STAMFORD STREET AND CHARING CROSS.

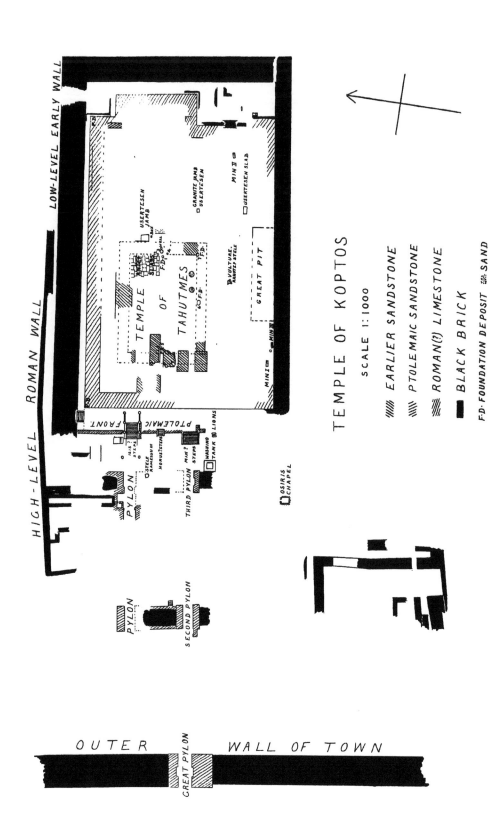

TEMPLE OF KOPTOS

SCALE 1:1000

///// EARLIER SANDSTONE

\\\\\ PTOLEMAIC SANDSTONE

///// ROMAN(?) LIMESTONE

■■ BLACK BRICK

F·D· FOUNDATION DEPOSIT ░░ SAND

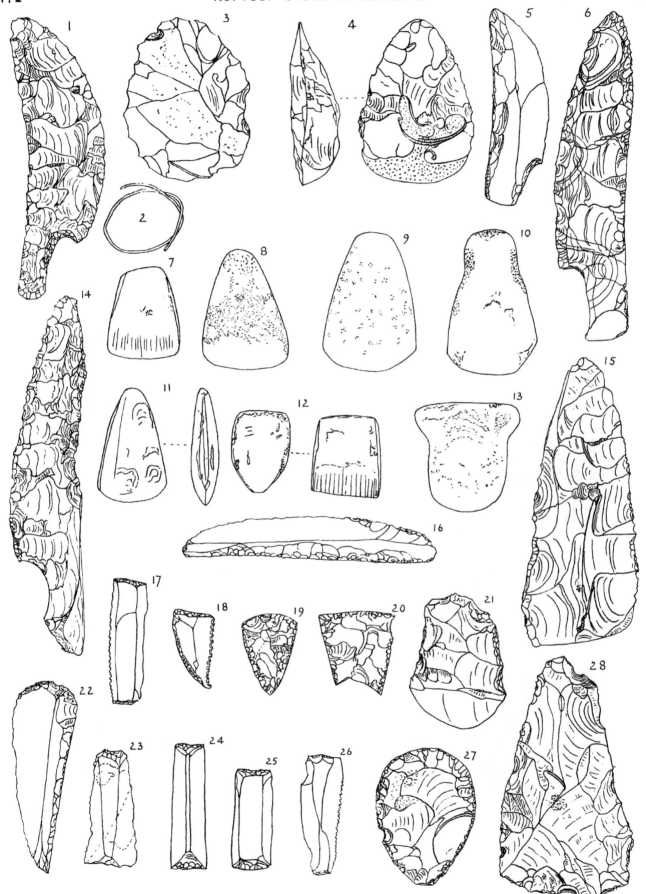

F.C.J.S.

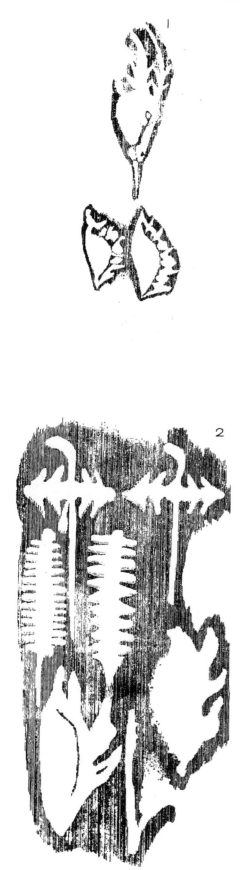

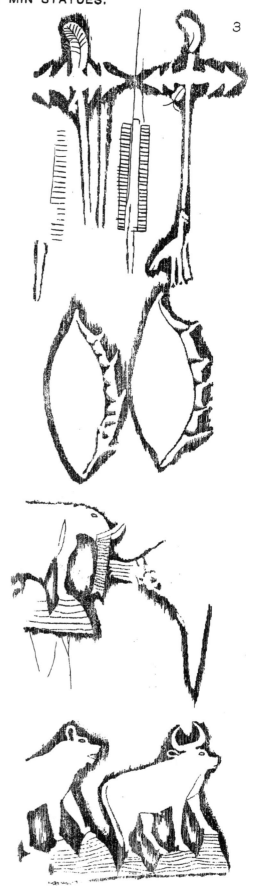

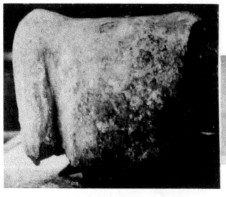

1 CHEST OF POTTERY FIGURE.

2 LOTUS GROUP AND DOG.

3 HIEROGLYPHS DEP ON STAND

4 HEAD OF MIN STATUE.

5 LION OF INVADERS VII DYN.

6 BIRD OF INVADERS VII. DYN.

7 PEPY II. & HATHOR HEADS.

8 PEPY II. STANDING.

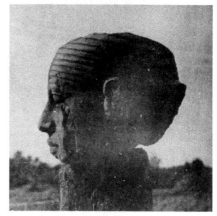

9 HEAD OF A KING (ANTEFP)

10 HEAD OF MIN. AMENEMHAT I.

11 HEAD OF LION. XII. OR XVIII. DYN.

12 OSIRIS WITH STARS. ROMAN.

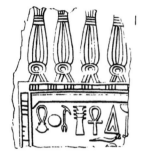

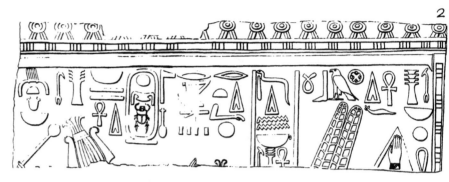

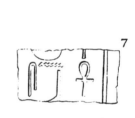

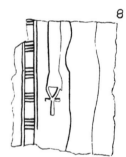

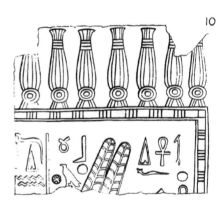

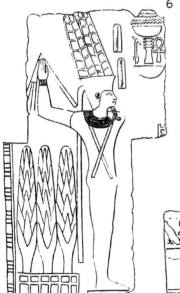

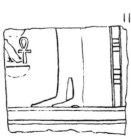

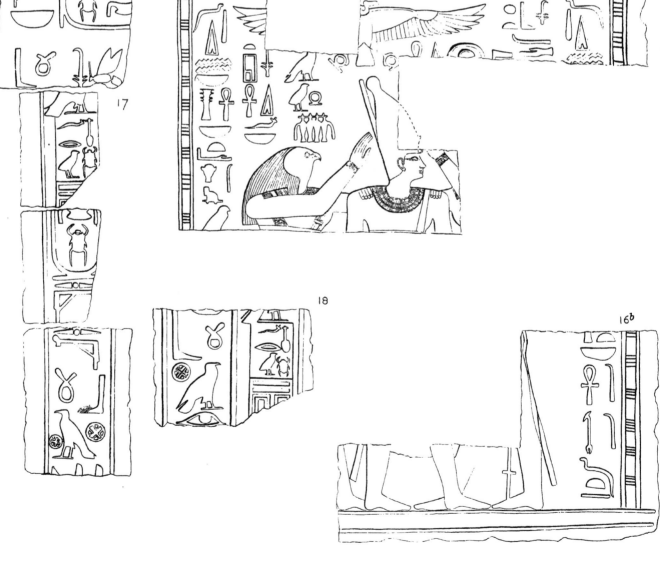

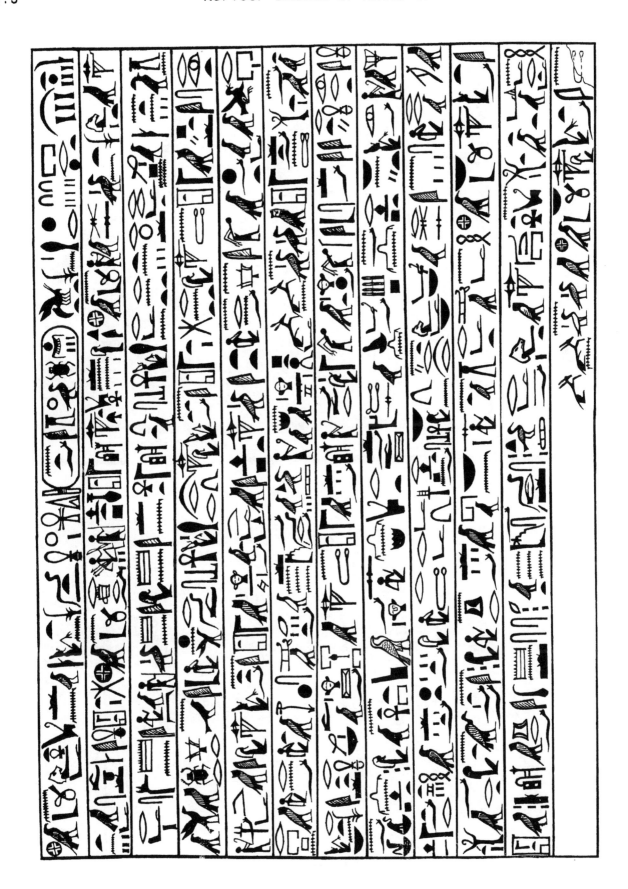

TEMPLE SCENE OF
AMENEMHATI & HIS KA
BEFORE MIN

TEMPLE SCENE OF
USERTESEN I
DANCING BEFORE MIN

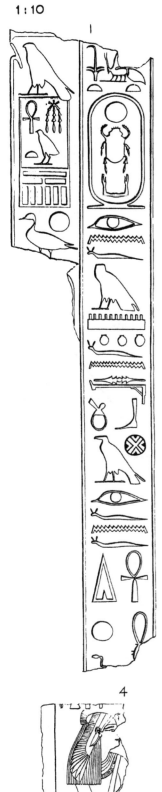

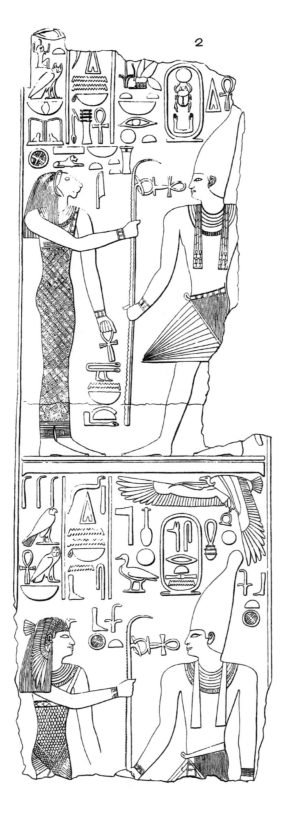

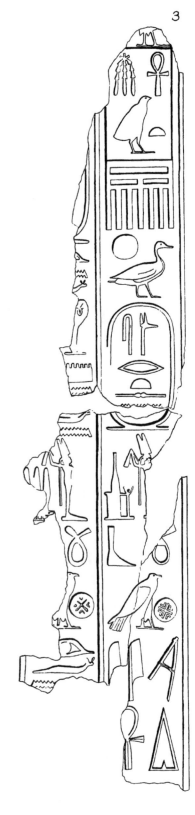

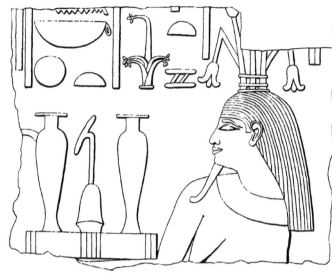

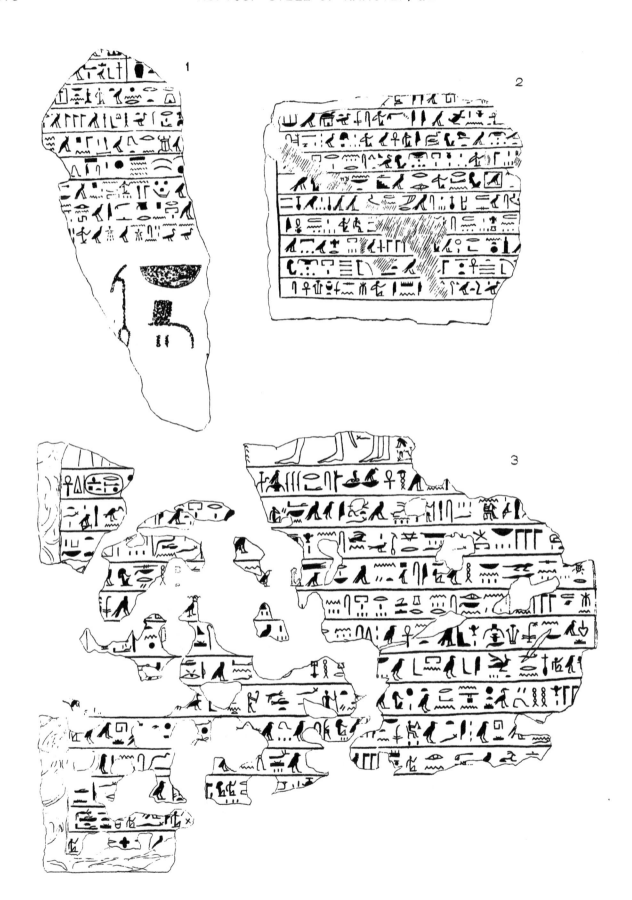

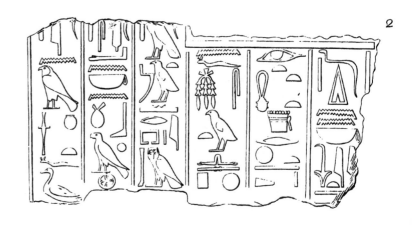

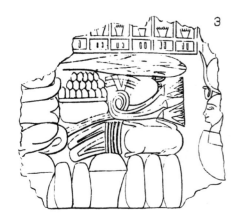

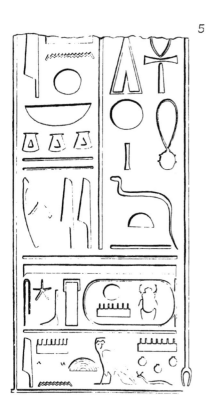

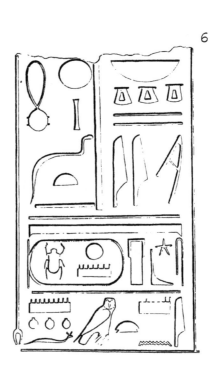

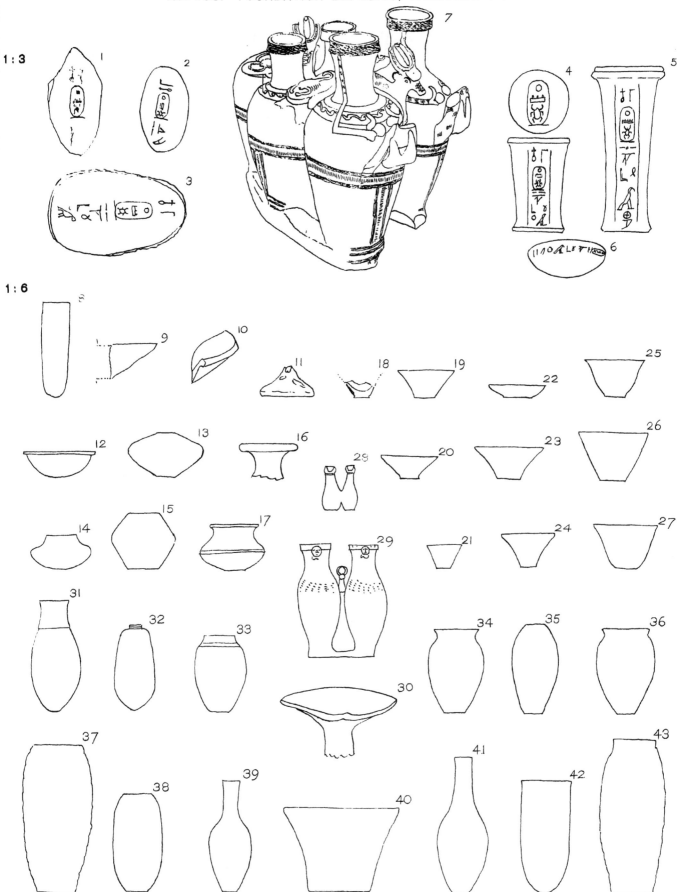

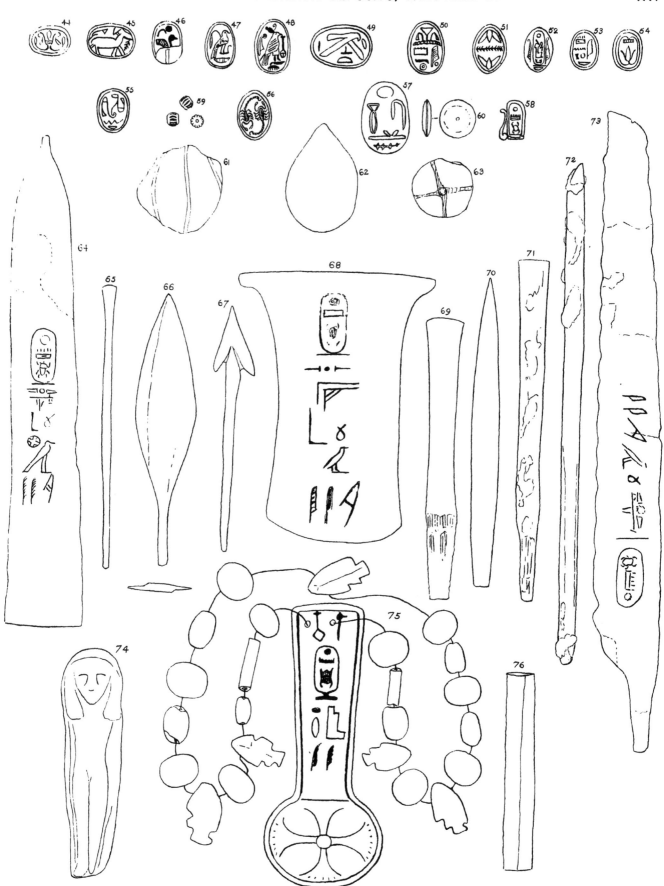

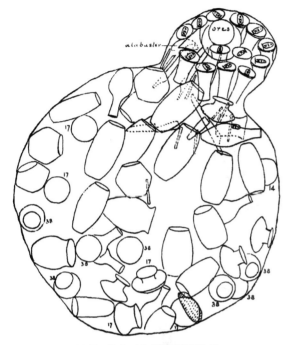

DEPOSIT Nº 7 OF TAHUTMES III

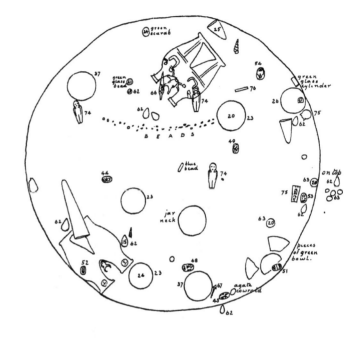

DEPOSIT Nº 3 OF TAHUTMES III.

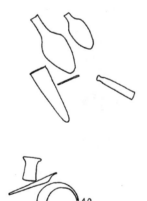

DEPOSIT Nº.1 OF TAHUTMES III

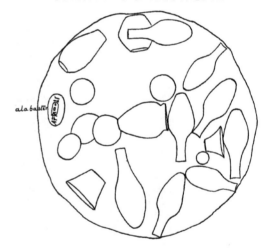

DEPOSIT Nº 2 OF TAHUTMES III

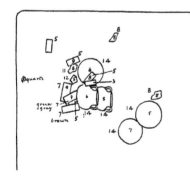

PTOLEMAIC DEPOSIT. N.W.

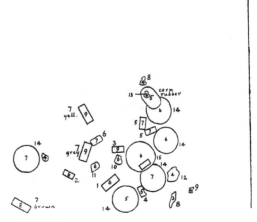

N.E. PTOLEMAIC DEPOSIT

1 : 10

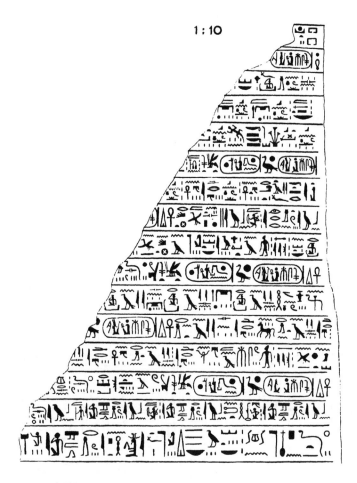

1 : 6

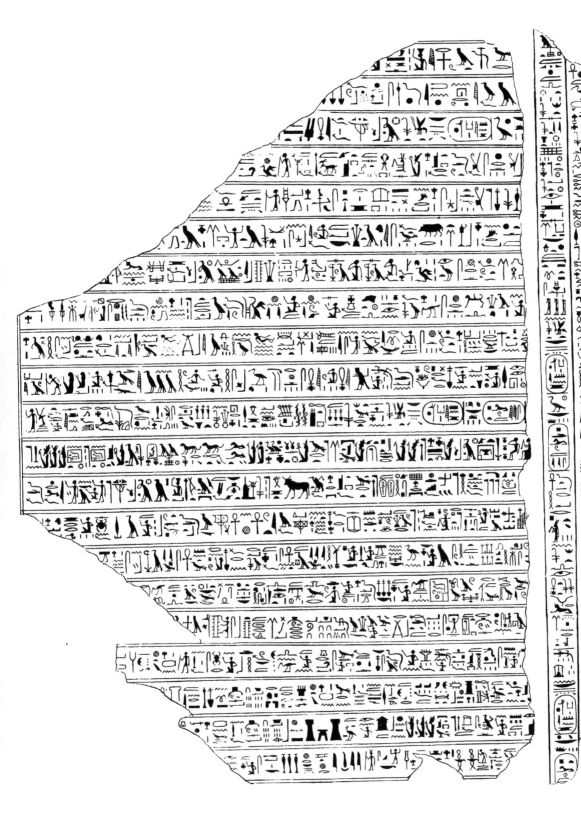

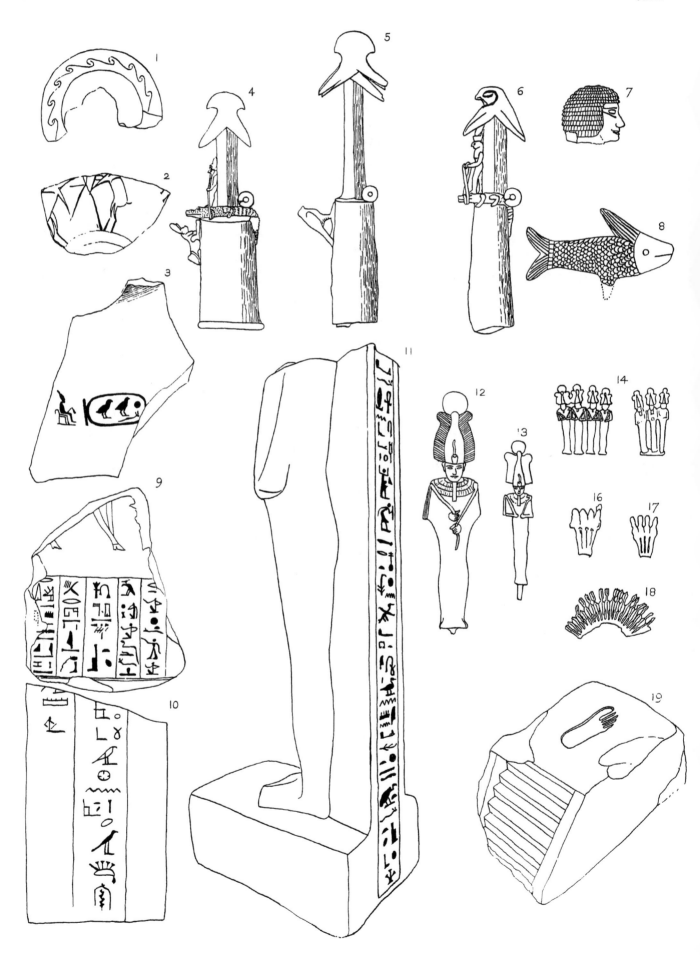

1 : 10

1 : 10

3 : 10

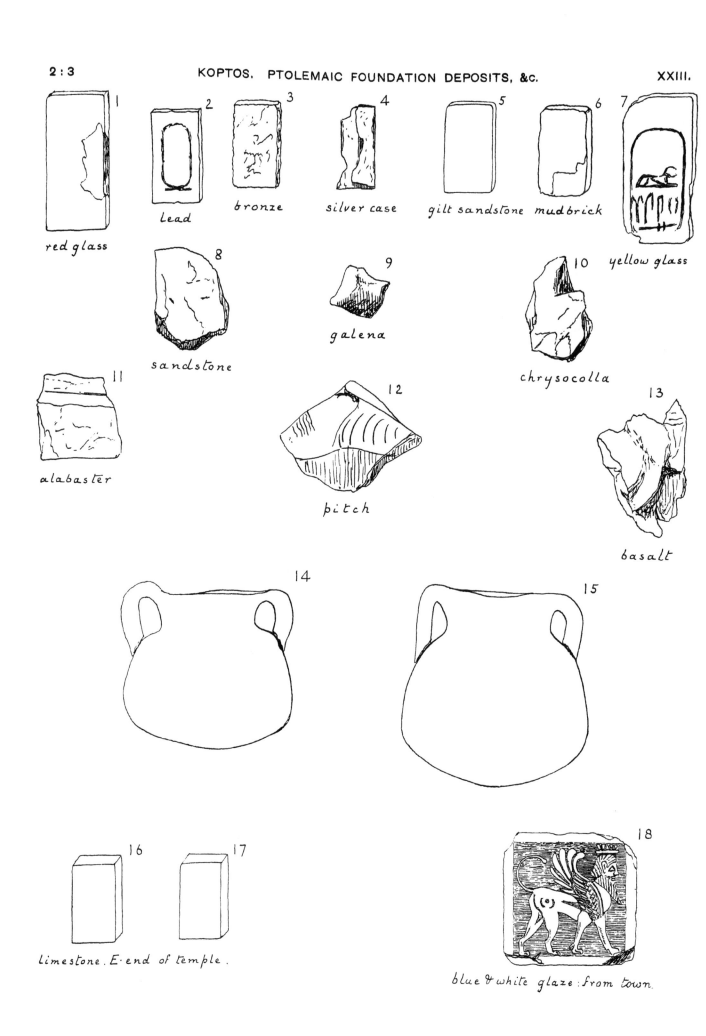

1 red glass

2 lead

3 bronze

4 silver case

5 gilt sandstone

6 mudbrick

7 yellow glass

8 sandstone

9 galena

10 chrysocolla

11 alabaster

12 pitch

13 basalt

14

15

16 17 limestone. E·end of temple.

18 blue & white glaze: from town.

1:1

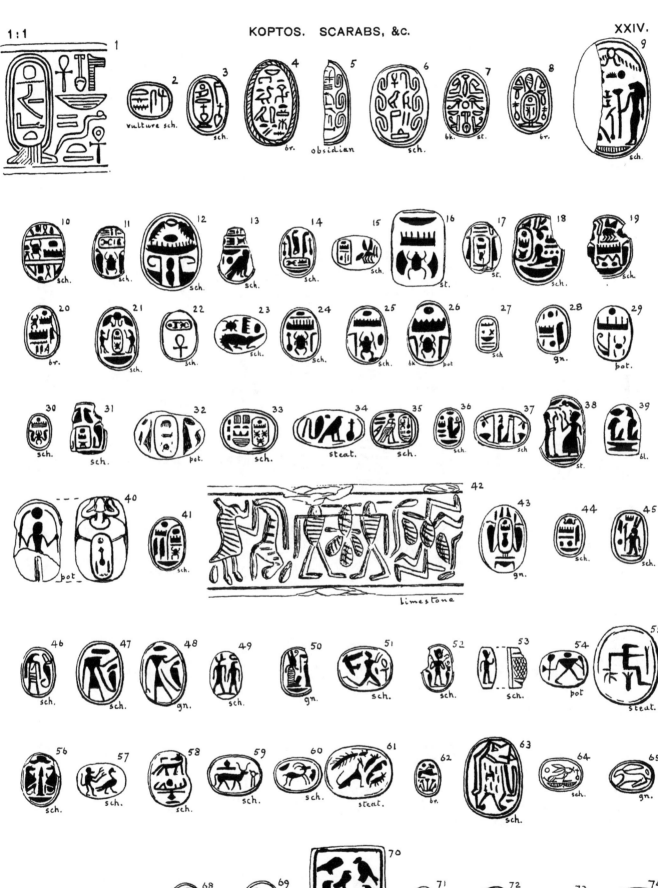

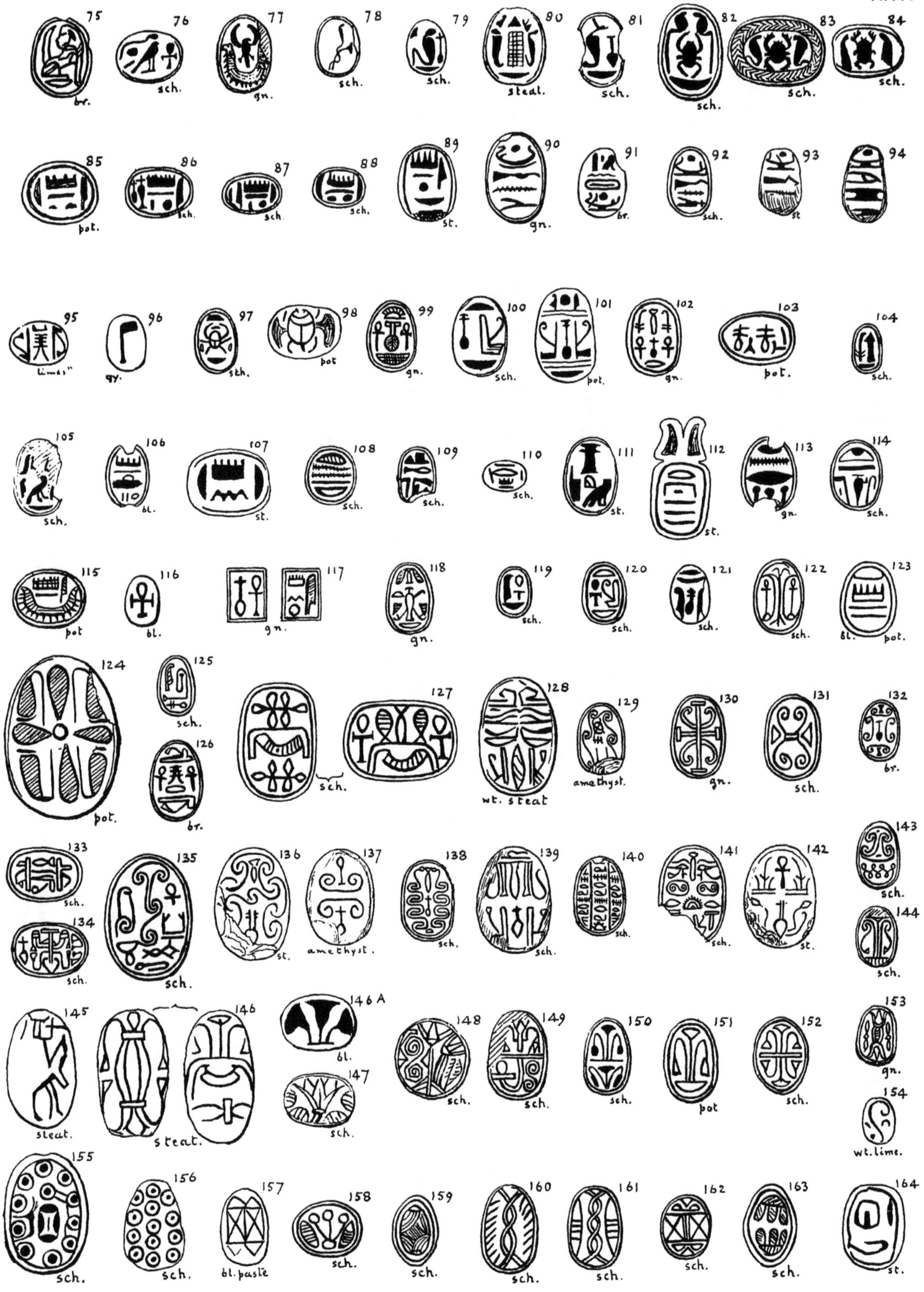
75 br.
76 sch.
77 gn.
78 sch.
79 sch.
80 steat.
81 sch.
82 sch.
83 sch.
84 sch.
85 pot.
86 sch.
87 sch.
88 sch.
89 st.
90 gn.
91 br.
92 sch.
93 st
94
95 limes"
96 qy.
97 sch.
98 pot
99 gn.
100 sch.
101 pot.
102 gn.
103 pot.
104 sch.
105 sch.
106 bl.
107 st.
108 sch.
109 sch.
110 sch.
111 st.
112 st.
113 gn.
114 sch.
115 pot
116 bl.
117 gn.
118 gn.
119 sch.
120 sch.
121 sch.
122 sch.
123 bl. pot.
124 pot.
125 sch.
126 br.
127 sch.
128 wt. steat
129 amethyst.
130 gn.
131 sch.
132 br.
133 sch.
134 sch.
135 sch.
136 st.
137 amethyst.
138 sch.
139 sch.
140 sch.
141 sch.
142 st.
143 sch.
144 sch.
145 steat.
146 steat.
146 A bl.
147 sch.
148 sch.
149 sch.
150 sch.
151 pot
152 sch.
153 gn.
154 wt. lime.
155 sch.
156 sch.
157 bl. paste
158 sch.
159 sch.
160 sch.
161 sch.
162 sch.
163 sch.
164 st.

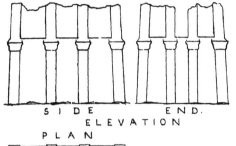

S I D E   E N D.

E L E V A T I O N

P L A N

R O M A N

B R I C K T O M B

SCALE 1/100

C O P T I C   B A P T I S T R Y

SCALE 1/250   GRANITE

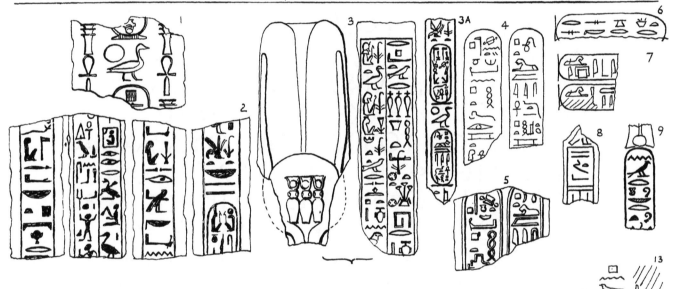

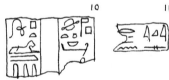

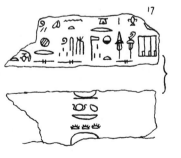

ΕΞ ΕΠΙ ΤΑΓΗ C /////////////////////////
/////////////////// ΟCΑ ΔΕΙ ΤΟΥ C ΜΙC Θω
ΤΑC ΤΟΥ ΕΝ ΚΟΠΤωΙ ΥΠΟΠ ΕΙΠΤΟ Ν
ΤΟC ΤΗ ΙΑ ΡΑ ΒΑΡΧΙΑ ΑΠΟCΤΟΛΙΟΥ ΠΡΑC
C ΕΙΝ ΚΑ ΤΑ ΤCΝ ΓΝ ωΜΟΝ ΛΤΗ ΔΕ ΤΗ
C ΤΗΛΗ ΙΕΝ Κ ΕΧΑΡΑΚ ΤΑΙ ΔΙΑ ΛΟΥ ΚΙΟΥ
ΑΝ ΤΙC ΤΙΟΥ ΑCΙΑ ΤΙΚΟΥ ΕΠΑΡΧΟΥ
ΟΡΟΥC ΒΕΡΕΝ CΙΚΗ C ////////////////
Ɑ ΚΥ ΒΕΡΝΗ ΤΟΥ CΡΥΘΡΑΙΚΟΥ ΔΡΑ
ΧΜΑC ΟΚ Τω
ΕΞ ΠΡωΡ ΕωC ΔΡΑΧΜΑC ΔΕ ΚΑ
/////////// ΑΚΟΥ ΔΡΑΧΜΑC ΔΕ ΚΑ
////////// ΚΥ ΤΟΥ ΔΡΑΧΜΑC ΠΕΝ ΤΕ
//////// Γ ΑΤΓ ΕΥ ΤΟΥ ΝΑΥΠΗΓΟΥ ΔΡΑΧΜΑC
ΠΕΝ ΤΕ ΧΕΙΡΟ ΤΕΧΝΟΥ ΔΡΑΧΜΑC
ΟΚΤω ΓΥΝΑΙΚωΝ ΠΡΟC Ε ΤΑΙΡΙC
ΜΟΝ ΔΡΑΧΜΑC ΕΚΑΤΟΝ ΟΚΤω
ΓΥΝΑΙΚωΝ ΕΙC ΠΛΕΟΥCωΝ ΔΡΑ
ΧΜΑC CΕΙΚΟCΙ ΓΥΝΑΙΚωΝ CΤΡΑΤΙ
ω ΤωΝ ΔΡΑΧΜΑC CΕΙΚΟCΙ
ΠΙΤΤΑΚΙΟΥ ΚΑΜΗΛωΝ ΟΒΟΛΟΝ ΕΝΑ
C ΦΡΑΓΙCΜΟΥ ΠΙΤΤΑΚΙΟΥ ΟΒΟΛΟΥC ΔΥΟ
ΠΟΡΕΙΑC ΕΞ ΕΡΧΟΜΕΝΗC ΕΚΑCΤΟΥ
ΠΙΤΤΑΚΙΟΥ ΤΟΥ ΑΝΔΡΟC ΑΝΑΒΑΙΝΟΝ
ΤΟC ΔΡΑΧΜΗΝ ΜΙΑΝ ΓΥΝΑΙΚωΝ
ΠΑCωΝ ΑΝΑ ΔΡΑΧΜΑC ΤΕCCΑΡΑC
ΟΝΟΥ ΟΒΟΛΟΥC ΔΥΟ ΑΜΑΞΗC ΕΧΟΥ
CΗ C ΤΕΤΡΑΓωΝΟΝ ΔΡΑΧΜΑC ΤΕCCΑΡΕC
ΙC ΤΟΥ ΔΡΑΧΜΑC CΕΙΚΟCΙ ΚΕΡΑΤΟC ΔΡΑ
ΧΜΑC ΤΕCCΑΡΕC ΤΑΦΗC ΑΝΑΦ ΕΡΟΜΕ
ΝΗC ΚΑΙ ΚΑΤΑΦ ΕΡΟΜΕΝΗC ΔΡΑΧΜΗΝ ΜΙ
ΑΝ ΤΕ ΤΡω ΒΟΛΟΝ ∟ Θ ΑΥΤΟΚΡΑΤΟΡΟC
ΚΑΙ CΑΡΟC ///////////// C CΕΒΑCΤΟΥ ////////// ΠΑΧω ΙC

1
ΕΩΙΜΕΓΙΣΤΩΙ
ΜΟΥΠΙΣ ΤΑΤΗΣ
ΘΕΑΣΙΣΙΔΟΣ
ΜΕΣΟΡΗΕΠΑΓΑ

2
L Β C ΕΓΟΥΙΟΥ ΓΑΛΒΑ ΑΥΤΟΚΑΤΟΡΟC
ΚΑΙCΑΡΟCCΕΒΑCΤΟΥ
ΜΗΝΟC ΝΕΟΥCΕΒΑCΤΟΥ
ΚΑ

3
IMP·CAESAR·T
CE//////////VS·PONTIF·MAXIMVS·TRIB·
POTEST·COS·XV·CENSOR·PERPETVS·P·P
PONTEM·A·SOLO·FECIT·

Q·LICINIO·ANCOTIO·PROCVIO·PRAEF·CAST
L·ANTISTIO·ASIATICO·PRAEF·BEREN·
CVRA·C·IVLI·MAGNI·ʒ·LEG·III·CYR

5
ΕΥCΕΒΙΑ ΛΑΡΙΝΕΙ
ΘΩΙ LΙΕ ΛΟΥΚΙΟΥ
CΕΠΤΙΜΙΟΥ CΕΟΥΗ
ΕΥCΕΒΟΥC ΠΕΡΤΙΝΑΚ
ΚΑΙ ΜΑΡΚΟΥ ΑΥΡΗΛΙΟΥ
ΑΝΤΩΝΙΝΟΥ ΕΥCΕΒΟΥC
CΕΒΑCΤΩΝ ΦΑΡΜ

7
ΥΠΕΡΔΙΑΜΟΝΗC
ΚΥΙΗΤΟΥCΕΒΑ
ΘΕΟΙCΤΟΤΕΜΕ
ΑΥΤΟΑΝΔΡΙΑC
ΑΡΕΙΟCΟΚΑΙC
ΒΟΥΛΕΥΤΗC
ΑΥΘΡΑΙΚΟCCΥ

8
ΘΕ ΜΕΓΙCΤΗ
ΙCΙΔΙ ΥΠΕΡ
ΕΥΠΛΟΙΑC
ΠΛΟΙΟΥCΑΡΑ
ΠΙΔΟC ΕΡΜΛΛ

6
ΕΤΟΥCΚΔ
ΤΟΥΚΥΡΙΟΥ
ΗΜΩΝΑΥΤΟΚΡΑΤΟΡΟ
CΕΟΥΗΡΟΥΑΝΤΩΝΙΝ
ΕΥCΕΒΟΥCΕΥΤΥΧΟΥC
CΕΒΑCΤΟΥΕΠΕΙΦΚ
ΘΕΩΜΕΓΙCΤΩΙΕΡΑΒ
ΛΩΜ ΑΥΡΗΛΙΟC
ΒΗΛΑΚΑΒΟCΙΕΡΕ
ΟΥΗCΙΛΛΑΡΙΟC
ΑΔΡΙΑΝΩΝΤΙΑΛΜ
ΡΗΙΩΝΑΝΤΩΝΙΝΙΑΝΩ
ΤΟΞΟΤΩΝ

9
ΠΟΥΩΝΞΑΡΠΑΗ
CΙCΑΝΕΘ⋕ΚΕΝΤΩ
ΙΔΙΩΘΕΩΙΜΕΓΙCΤ

11
ΑΡΔΙΩΑΤΤΟ
ΟΥCΜΑΥΡΗΛΙΟCCΕ
ΝΙCΒΤΟΝΝΑΟΝΟΙΚΟ
ΕΖΩΓΡΑΦΗCΕΝΤΗΝ
ΘΙΝΕΠΟΙΗCΕΝΕΚΤΟΥ
ΤΟΠΡΟCΚΥΝΗΜΑΝ
ΒΩΕΠΑΘΙ

12
ΙΟΝ ΜΕΓΑΝ
ΛΟΚΑΙCΑΡΑ

ΡΝΥCΙΟC
ΚΟΠ
ΤΗC

10
ΑΡΙCΤΟΝΕΙΚΟCΔΙΔΥ
ΛΑΔΕΛΦΟCΕΡΩΝΙ
ΠΤΑΜΗΝΙ⋕ΕΝ
ΕΥΨΥΧΕΙ

CΑΤΟΥΡΝΕΙΝΟΥ

13
ΤΟΠΟCΑΡΙCΤΙΟΥ CΑΤΟΥΡ ΝΕΙΝΟΥ ΕΠΑ ΘΩΙ ΑΡΙCΤΙ

QURNEH. SITHATHOR TOMB. XVII DYNASTY?
FESTIVAL SCENE OF SINGERS AND DANCERS.

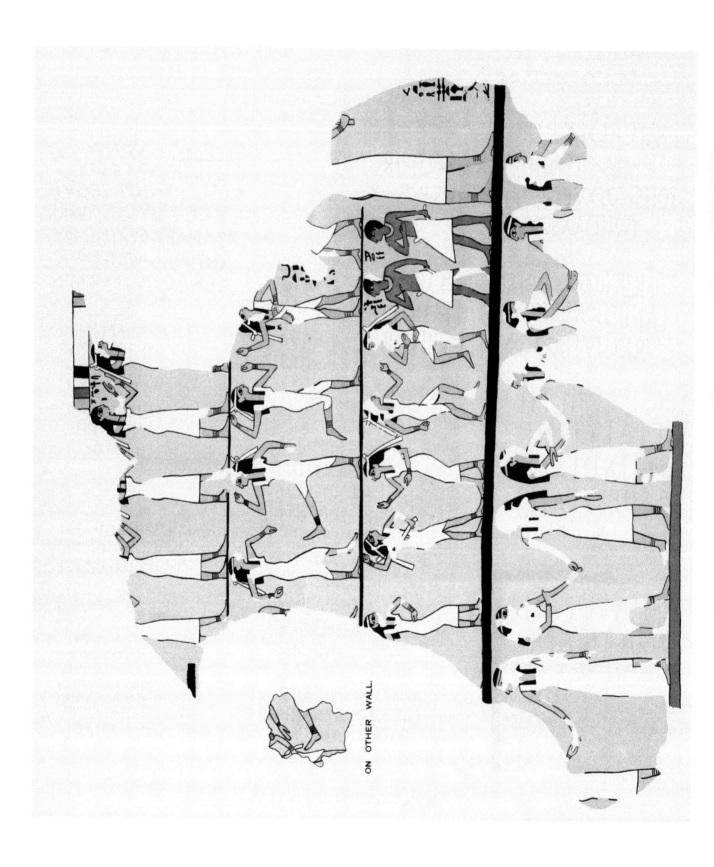

ON OTHER WALL.

BRITISH SCHOOL OF ARCHAEOLOGY IN EGYPT
AND EGYPTIAN RESEARCH ACCOUNT
FIFTEENTH YEAR, 1909

QURNEH

BY

W. M. FLINDERS PETRIE

Hon. D.C.L., LL.D., Litt.D., Ph.D.
F.R.S., F.B.A., Hon. F.S.A. (Scot.)
MEMBER OF THE ROYAL IRISH ACADEMY
MEMBER OF THE IMPERIAL GERMAN ARCHAEOLOGICAL INSTITUTE
CORRESPONDING MEMBER OF THE SOCIETY OF ANTHROPOLOGY, BERLIN
MEMBER OF THE ROMAN SOCIETY OF ANTHROPOLOGY
MEMBER OF THE SOCIETY OF NORTHERN ANTIQUARIES
MEMBER OF THE AMERICAN PHILOSOPHICAL SOCIETY
EDWARDS PROFESSOR OF EGYPTOLOGY, UNIVERSITY OF LONDON

WITH A CHAPTER BY
Dr. J. H. WALKER

LONDON
SCHOOL OF ARCHAEOLOGY IN EGYPT
UNIVERSITY COLLEGE, GOWER STREET, W.C.
AND
BERNARD QUARITCH
11, GRAFTON STREET, NEW BOND STREET, W.
1909

PRINTED BY
HAZELL, WATSON AND VINEY, LD.,
LONDON AND AYLESBURY.

BRITISH SCHOOL OF ARCHAEOLOGY IN EGYPT, AND EGYPTIAN RESEARCH ACCOUNT

The need of providing for the training of students is even greater in Egypt than it is in Greece and Italy; and the relation of England to Egypt at present makes it the more suitable that support should be given to a British School in that land. This body is the only such agency, and is also the basis of the excavations of Prof. Flinders Petrie, who has had many students associated with his work in past years. The great enterprise of the excavation of the temples and city of Memphis, which has now been undertaken, promises the most valuable results. But it will necessarily be far more costly than any other work in Egypt, and it cannot be suitably carried out without increasing the present income of the School. Active support is required to ensure the continuance of such work, which depends entirely on personal contributions, and each subscriber receives the annual volume. The antiquities not retained by the Egyptian Government are presented to Public Museums, after the Annual Exhibition, during July, at University College. The accounts are audited by a Chartered Accountant, and published in the Annual Report. Treasurer: H. SEFTON-JONES.

ADDRESS THE HON. SECRETARY,
BRITISH SCHOOL IN EGYPT, UNIVERSITY COLLEGE,
GOWER STREET, LONDON, W.C.

CONTENTS

LIST OF PLATES

WITH PAGE REFERENCES TO THE DESCRIPTIONS

QURNEH

INTRODUCTION

1. THE work of the earlier part of the season was at Qurneh, the northern end of the cemetery of Thebes on the western side. It was carried on from 9 December 1908 to 8 February 1909, after which the workmen from Quft were moved down to Memphis, to continue the work there in the dry end of the season. On such a site as Qurneh a short spell of work could not achieve any large systematic clearance. The main subject was a search in some of the desert valleys for the possible discovery of any remote tombs. Two small valleys were searched; one by trenching the whole of the likely surfaces, with the result of finding one fine interment of the XVIIth dynasty; the other valley was cleared deep and wide over the most promising parts without any result. Another complete work was the clearing of a new temple site of the XIXth dynasty. An important discovery at the close of the time was the *Sed* festival chapel of Sankh-ka-ra of the XIth dynasty; some more clearance might be made there, but as it is on the top of the mountain three miles away, we only spent two days on it. The northern end of the cemetery in the plain opposite Karnak was searched as long as anything could be found, with the result of getting a large collection of pottery of the XIth dynasty, here published, and an important historical inscription. And a little was done on the Drah abul Nega hill, both in copying tombs and finding objects. Most of the ground we touched will not need to be looked at again; but two months' work is as nothing in the exploration of such a site.

2. The structure of the western hills at Thebes is but little known; though thousands of persons visit the Tombs of the Kings, hardly any one has seen the other valleys, and the usual maps do not include them. As this was our district, I made a sketch plan of the valleys, given in Pl. IV. The principal peaks were triangulated from a base in the plain; positions at every half-mile or so were fixed by compass-bearings to these triangulated points; and then the hillsides were sketched from all these positions. The plan is probably correct to one or two hundred feet in any part over the three miles' extent. The contours are mostly at the abrupt cliff lines which run around the hills (see Pl. V); and the levels of these main hard strata are about 1200 feet, 1000, 750, and a plateau of 300 to 400 feet. These heights, and some others noted on the plan, were taken approximately by the angular height, as reflected in water.

The expression of the plan is by assuming a top left-hand shadow, as from an afternoon sun in the south-west. The cliff lines facing east and north are then in deep shadow, shewn here by thick contours. In looking at the map it should be imagined as a relief model in layers, lighted from the top left. The stream lines, or valley bottoms, are marked by arrows.

The whole structure may be called a horse-shoe basin draining to the east, with a great peak on each side of it. The southern peak is the well-known point above the Theban cemetery; the northern peak is two miles away, that of Sankh-ka-ra. Up the middle of the horse-shoe is a ridge dividing it in two, and up this ridge runs the road to the high desert plateau, a short cut to Farshut, thirty-six miles distant. On the west the tableland is cut off by a great valley about four miles wide, which runs in from the Birket Habu northward; and the Far-shut road turns north and skirts round the head of this valley.

Various walls of rough stone have been built to prevent easy access from the sides into the northern valley, and many stone shelters and sentry-walks guard the neck south of Sankh-ka-ra. Another long sentry-go guards the ridge above the Tombs of the Kings from being reached by the Farshut road. At S and S by the path leading up to Sankh-ka-ra are seats of palaeolithic man, smooth clearances on the ground with great numbers of worked flints around.

On many parts of the hills most of the flints have been broken artificially in trying them for tool-making; and the work is clearly palaeolithic. The forts marked at the mouth of the largest valley are small square rooms; the southern is thirteen feet square, the northern twenty-five feet square, outside. The date must be late Roman, as a piece of a ribbed amphora of about the IVth century A.D. was found in a brick: and the sizes of the bricks are too small for earlier dates.

3. The party engaged on this work was four in number. Mr. Mackay was there from the first preliminaries to the end of the packing; I was there during the whole of the excavating; my wife stayed for seven weeks drawing tomb-scenes, temple-scenes, and pottery; and Mr. Wainwright superintended part of the men for a month, after which he did drawings of the foreigners in tombs, and went to Memphis to start some of the work there. As visitors we had Mr. Hatton, and Dr. and Mrs. Seligmann who stayed a fortnight for anthropological enquiries.

CHAPTER I

THE ANTEF CEMETERY.

4. To the north of the stream-bed that runs down from the Tombs of the Kings a low stretch of desert is spread out, containing a cemetery of pit and portico tombs, for about half a mile along the desert edge. This is divided in two by a little channel; the north half we noted as cemetery A, the south half as cemetery B. Besides these there are a few tombs noted as N, from being under the temple of Nebunnef further to the south. As a whole, cemetery A was mostly clear of burials later than the XIth dynasty; while cemetery B had been much re-used in the XXIInd—XXVIth dynasties.

The range of time of the first use of these cemeteries is so short that not much can be traced of changes in the tombs or the pottery. Regarding the direction of the tombs those in B are nearly all north of east, while in A they are equally north and south of east. Which is the earlier class is indicated by the jars with brims, Nos. 554–96 on Pl. XX, a class which is well known to descend from the Old Kingdom (see *Dendereh*), to the XIth dynasty (see *Gizeh and Rifeh* XIII, A to D) and to become extinct in the XIIth dynasty. Now these occur in eight north-east tombs in cemetery B, in four north-east tombs in cemetery A, and in not one south-east

tomb. Hence the north-east direction is the earlier, and half of cemetery A is later than cemetery B. The north-east tombs were reckoned as north, and the south-east as facing east. These differ from the directions at Dendereh and Hu, see *Diospolis*, p. 43.

A fixed point is given by the group of pottery on Pl. XIII, which was found in a tomb with the steles naming Uah-ankh Antef. This tomb does not contain any brim jar (554–96), nor any wavy mouths (283–354), nor any kohl pottery (263–82); but we can trace its relation to these distinctive classes. The other tombs with which the Antef group is connected by similar forms are A 7, 12?, 15, 24, 26, 32, 47, 54 and B 5, 8, 12, 14, 26?, 33, 40. Of these tombs three (A 7, 15, 26) also have jars, shewing that such extend to the Antef period. Further, the wavy mouths which are common in the XIIth dynasty are found with the jars (in A 7, 18, 23, 27, 28, 39; B 2, 16, 19, 34), but are only found in two tombs (A 7, B 8) with pottery like the Antef forms. And A 7 is the only tomb in which Antef forms are associated with kohl pottery. Hence we may conclude that brim jars (554–96) extend far beyond the Antef age, that wavy mouths (283–354) were scarcely beginning then, and that kohl pottery (263–82) was probably not earlier than the XIIth dynasty. As more than half the groups of pottery contain wavy mouths, which are scarcely as early as Antef,—and one in six contain kohl pottery, which is certainly later, and probably of the XIIth dynasty,—the general conclusion is that most of these tombs are of the latter half of the XIth and early in the XIIth dynasty. Probably the change of direction to south of east is due to the XIIth dynasty.

5. The form of the tombs with pottery was usually a long pit, with length averaging 90 inches in earlier and 87 in later times, breadth 33 in earlier, 27 in later, depth 108 in earlier and 132 in later times. The classes of earlier and later are separated by the absence or presence of wavy mouths and kohl pottery. These pits had usually a chamber at each end, and the chambers show no difference between the periods, averaging 95 to 97 inches in length and width, and 36 inches in height. Altogether 48 tombs were measured. Only five bodies remained, of which four lay on the left side and one on the right.

Of the skulls, sixty-five were collected and measured; the sex of each was estimated by the appearance. The median dimensions in millimetres are, length (Broca) 183·5 m., 178 f.; breadth max. 135 m., 130 f.; bizygomatic 126·5 m., 121 f.; biauricular 116 m., 112 f.; height (bregma), 138 m., 130·5 f.; basi-nasal 101·5 m., 97 f.; basi-alveolar 98·5 m., 94·5 f.; nasi-alveolar 69·5 m., 65·5 f.; nasal height 51 m., 47·5 f.; nasal width 25·5 m., 25 f.; nasi-maxillary height of face 115 m., 111 f.; lower maxillary height to meeting of teeth 40·5 m., 40·2 f.; maxillary length 116 m., 110·5 f.; maxillary breadth low 92·5 m., 92 f., at joint 113·5 m., 109 f. The nasi-maxillary height, from the nasion to the chin, gives the facial height; and the 'maxillary height gives the position of the mouth. With the bizygomatic breadth, they give the proportions of the face. The height of the jaws, upper and lower, shews no certain difference of sex, only the nasal height affects the greater height of the male face.

Beside the pit tombs with chambers, described above, there were also many portico tombs. A court-yard was cut into the slope of the hard gravel; and then a chamber or a series of chambers was cut into the vertical face, with often a portico of pillars left in front of the chambers. These had nearly all been plundered in various past times, and only in one of these larger tombs was anything found. The tomb No. 2, Pl. XI, had the two Antef steles lying in the doorway, and the pottery Pl. XIII in the chamber itself. The plans, measured and drawn by Mr. Mackay, were selected as the best examples of different types; but the gravel conglomerate is so rough that no precision of measurement is possible. A similar tomb was found at Dendereh belonging to the same age, of a man Antefaqer, and published in *Dendereh*, Pl. XXXIII.

In these tombs are various types (Pl. XI). (1) A single chamber with a pillar in the middle to support the gravel roof. (2) Two entrances to a corridor, with a passage out of the end of it to a small chamber, in which is the funeral pit. (3) A portico with two pillars, a chamber off the end of it, and a larger chamber at the back of it, with the funeral pit in the corner. (4) A long portico of ten pillars, with a chamber behind it, and a smaller chamber behind that containing the pit. (5) A long gallery with side recesses, one of which contains the pit. (6) A long gallery with side chambers, and a branch from it with other chambers. There is a great variety of the forms, and in some cases there are two or more entrances behind the portico, and secondary porticoes on the other sides of the courtyard. Most of these tombs are so much wrecked and fallen in that the plan is difficult to complete.

The inscriptions found in the cemetery will be dealt with by Dr. Walker in the last chapter. Here we may note that the two tablets of Zara found together refer separately to his family position and his official position; both allude to the Horus Uah-ankh Antef. The conquest of Abydos by that king was already known from the royal stele; and we here read that Zara protected the land as far north as Aphroditopolis, fifty miles north of Abydos.

6. The beads and kohl vases found in the cemetery are of early types agreeing with the age of the pottery. We will here note them in groups, according to the pottery that was found with them. In these plates the reference numbers on the right are to A cemetery, and those on the left to B cemetery. With the brim jars, and therefore perhaps of the earlier age, there are the tombs A 6 with the double limestone kohl tube VIII, 27; A 16 with the well-formed alabaster kohl vase VIII, 10; A 19 the spiral beads of large size, VIII, 28, an indigo ball bead, 30, and a sandstone sharpener, 29; B 23 the bird vase of black pottery, XII, 3 (see also Pl. IX), and the beads, XII, 8; lastly B 24 with the alabaster vase VIII, 23. The tombs with jars and also wavy mouths are late XIth or XIIth dynasty, such are A 18 with the alabaster kohl vase VIII, 6, and beads, 7; and B 19 with the rough scarab XII, 15, and beads, 16, 7. The tombs with wavy-mouth vases of late XIth or XIIth dynasty are A 5 with beads XII, 9; B 10 with pink limestone vase VIII, 19; B 20 with rounded alabaster vase VIII, 9, pieces of pottery box with hieratic inscription of Ransenb, and pottery head XXXI, 3, perhaps from a canopic vase; in B 30 was the pottery doll, XXXI, 6; and in B 33 the broken stele Pl. X. The last class of tombs are those with the little drab pottery kohl pots, which are quite disconnected from the Antef tomb, and almost certainly of the XIIth dynasty. These are A 8 with large ball beads and spiral beads, VIII, 17, 18; A 14 with beads XII, 7, and mirror XXXI, 2; A 21 with alabaster vase VIII, 20, beads 22, and sandstone 21; A 31 with pink and grey hard limestone vase, VIII, 4; and A 56 with alabaster vase, and small beads of carnelian and blue glaze, VIII, 1, 2. There is nothing in this last class which is outside of the XIIth dynasty, and some things clearly belong to that time.

7. Next we may note the groups which are not dated by distinctive pottery. A 4 seems to be before the XIth dynasty, perhaps of the VIIIth or IXth, as the carnelian uraeus (XII, 5) is like the Old Kingdom amulets, and likewise the little figure of glaze. The

blue glazed pot, VIII, 12, is also like those made at the close of the Old Kingdom, the alabaster VIII, 11 and bone tool, 13, accompanied it. The rosette scarab of A 15 (XII, 12) inherits the geometric style of the VIth—VIIIth dynasties, but the pottery with it is connected with the Antef group. Apparently of the XIIth dynasty is A 9 with two carnelian beads and pottery, shewn here as a group, 632–6, 637 being apparently of a later burial; also A 33 with characteristic XIIth dynasty vase, beads, and ink-slab, VIII, 14, 15, 16; and probably A 45 is of the same age, XII, 18, 19.

The dating of the pottery we have already considered, but some notes may be added about the plates for easier reference. Pl. XIII gives the best group known for dating the XIth dynasty pottery: it is absolutely fixed to the time of Uah-ankh Antef by the steles found with it, Pls. II, III. On comparing these with the pottery which was approximately dated at Rifeh, Nos. 8–9 are like 97 and 104 Rifeh types, and 19 like 121 Rifeh, there dated as Xth or XIth dynasty; while 14 is like 174 Rifeh and 28 like 177 Rifeh, there dated to XIth or XIIth dynasties (see Gizeh and Rifeh, Pls. XIII C, D). Thus the rougher dating before agrees fairly with the precise dating now to Antef. In general the forms which at Rifeh were put to the Xth dynasty 62, 77, 78, may be compared with Nos. 386, 566, 554 here; the forms of the Xth or XIth dynasties, 81, 83, 131, 136, 138 Rifeh, are like Nos. 168, 563, 603, 577, 566 here; and the forms of the XIth or XIIth dynasties, 172, 174, 192, 193 Rifeh, are like Nos. 249, 502, 477, 400 here.

In Pl. XIV the forms of the saucers and bowls are not so distinctive as other types. In Pl. XV the bowls with lips turned down, 161–5, are of the wavy-mouth group of the next plate. The bowls 167–70 belong to the IXth—Xth dynasty style. The class of smooth light red pottery 247–52 is difficult to date; at first it looks like the early XVIIIth dynasty style, but there seems no sufficient reason for double-dating all these tombs. It stands at present quite apart in paste, in colour, and the use of crimson on the top edge. The scrabbled patterns on 256–8 are well known in the XIIth dynasty.

In Pl. XVI the little drab kohl pottery, 263–82, is well known in the XIIth dynasty; and it is probably here of that age, as it is detached from the Antef group and from the tombs connected with that. The wavy-mouth forms, 283–354, also belong to the XIIth dynasty, but as they link here to the Antef

group, they probably begin in the XIth. The spouted vases 355–9 are always associated with the previous types, and of the same age. Pl. XVII shews the forms leading in to the globular types. Pl. XVIII is entirely of a class of rough pots which are very common, but varied in details. The higher-shouldered forms are at the top, the most baggy at the bottom, the straightest at the left hand, the most rounded at the right.

Pl. XIX shews the drooping forms, wider at the base. At the bottom are the stands, and a small group from under the Nebunnef temple, N 1, which seems to be of the XIIth dynasty, compare 550 with Rifeh 164. Pl. XX shews the class of brim jars which descend from the Old Kingdom, but are shewn here to extend probably into the XIIth dynasty. The cellular dish 597 is a new form. The type of lid 598 covered with white spots is already known. We now begin the trays of offerings, connected with the soul-houses (see Gizeh and Rifeh XIV). Two small groups, N 2, and N 3, are from under the Nebunnef temple. The trays on Pl. XXI are of the roughest forms known. In connection with these we may refer to the photograph, Pl. LIII, of a group of modern soul-houses, piled together by a large stone in the mouth of the valley of the Tombs of the Kings. This stone marks the burial of a holy man, jars of water are put for his refreshment, and soul-houses for his soul to come and rest in. One has even the staircase like the ancient forms. It is very striking to see that the custom of offering model houses for the soul, such as we found at Rifeh of the IXth—XIIth dynasties, is still continued in modern times.

CHAPTER II

THE CHAPEL OF SANKH-KA-RA, XITH DYNASTY.

8. THE mass of hill and valley behind Qurneh is but little known beyond the immediate region of the Tombs of the Kings, and our main purpose was to explore a part of it. On Pl. IV will be seen the general plan of the great denudation valleys which occupy this area. The plan should be viewed as showing the shadows of a relief model in steps, following the main precipices of the cliffs, at about 1200, 1000, 750, and 300 to 400 feet above the plain: the sun is supposed to be in the south-west, at the top left hand, north being to the right hand, as the ground is viewed from the plain. The two leading features of the region are the peaks left one on either

side of the great horse-shoe hollow of denudation. That on the south is the great peak of Thebes above the cemetery; while two miles north of it is an even higher peak marked here as Sankh-ka-ra chapel, and photographed on Pl. V.

Some years ago Dr. Spiegelberg visited the summit, and found brick walls, which he considered to be a temple of Thoth, and by that name it is officially known. Dr. Schweinfurth also ascended it; but all I could hear from residents was that there were some Coptic walls on it. Yet it is by no means inaccessible. From where we lived at Qurneh it is only 25 minutes' walk to the foot, and 45 minutes' climb up the 1200 feet; while returning only takes 50 minutes in all. On going to the top I saw that it was clearly an old Egyptian shrine or small temple, as may be seen by the views given on Pl. V. Accordingly a few workmen were taken up, and the rubbish in the chapel itself was turned over. Besides the chapel I noticed some building behind it, and on a later day we cleared the plan of it, and found two halls each with eight stone bases. Some further clearance in front of the chapel produced nothing.

9. The plan of the chapel is given on Pl. VI. It is a temenos enclosure, 70 feet 3 inches by 80 feet 8 inches over all. Outside of that is a scarp along the two sides, built up of rough stones, to support a platform round the temenos, and a scarp in front with a gangway left in it. Inside the temenos is the chapel, a square block of building with three cells at the back of it. Under the floor-level are low walls of rough stone, with a rather different plan; and in front of the left cell is a step down remaining from over the low wall, plastered and whitened like the general walls and floor. The cells therefore were below the floor-level of the chapel. In the back of the left cell are two niches in the wall where cupboards were probably placed for the deposit of small property. The front of the middle and right cells has been broken away. These low walls before the cells are certainly earlier, and seem as if they had belonged to a preliminary structure.

10. The remains found in the chapel are shown on Pl. VII. There is a long column of royal titles and names of Sankh-ka-ra, which is shewn (by the section at the base) to have projected from a block of limestone. At the side of this is part of a similar column of inscription, adjoining a roll moulding. These show that a large block of limestone was carved with roll moulding down the edges, and narrow pilasters.

Further, pieces were found of what is clearly a sarcophagus lid, well finished outside, roughly hollowed inside, of which the section is in the middle of Pl. VII. Along the curved top were many graffiti, shewn at the side of it; and along the cornice edge and top were other graffiti shewn at the top of the plate. One large flat surface has a graffito, shewn at the left base of the plate. And at the base are also some chips of a small finely cut original inscription. Above this is shewn a fragment of a seated figure, half life-size. It is the knee with the left hand resting on it, and a close-fitting tunic coming down over the wrist.

The presence of many graffiti of successive visitors upon the loose lid shews that it stood where it was accessible, and not in a tomb pit. The name of Senusert shews that it was visited and still complete in the XIIth dynasty. We must then picture a cenotaph or imitation sarcophagus, with roll moulding, pilaster framing, and a separate lid with cornice, standing freely accessible in the chapel, where there is no trace of a well or tomb pit. And along with it was a seated figure in Osiride dress as worn at the Sed festival. The limestone cenotaph was not merely a niche or shrine for the figure, or it would not have had a separate lid, well finished at the joint and rough underneath. That lid proves that a cenotaph sarcophagus existed, the inside of which was invisible.

The column of inscription has first the Horus name, S-ankh-taui-f, "making his two lands to live"; the vulture-and-uraeus name has not been recovered; the Horus on nubti name is hotep, not previously known; the throne name Sankh-ka-ra has not been recovered; but the personal name Mentu-hotep is preserved. Probably the fragment of "Hathor lady of . . ." belonged to this column or one similar, as there is no roll at the outer edge of it. There seem to have been adorations to the various gods by Sankh-ka-ra, of which we have fragments to Hathor and Horus.

11. Some years ago I pointed out in *Researches in Sinai* (p. 181) how the *Sed* feast was the Osirification of the king, when his successor was nominated, after which the king reigned as Osiris until his death. This was the modified form of a custom of killing the king at a fixed period, such as is known in modern times both in Africa and India (see Frazer, *Lectures on the Kingship*, 293). The earliest scenes of this feast, before and during the Ist dynasty, shew the king enthroned as Osiris in a shrine and his successor dancing the sacred dance before him;

other men also took part in the dance, which seems to have been held in a curtained enclosure, the emblem of which survived in the three hemi-discs placed behind the king in the dancing scene. The royal daughters were brought to the feast, probably to be married to the successor, who was not the king's son in early times. This Osirification of the king is well known in scenes of Pepy and other early kings, seated clothed in a tunic, covering down to the wrists. The seated figure of a king Mentuhotep clothed in such a tunic was found buried in a pit at Thebes, by Mr. Carter; and this is the Osiride figure of the deified king, buried as deceased at his Sed feast.

Now the seated figure of Sankh-ka-ra here was clothed likewise in the tunic down to the hands. It was an Osiride figure of the deified king. And the cenotaph, or imitation sarcophagus, of which we have verified the lid and inscriptions, would have represented the burial of the human nature of the king, in place of the actual killing and funeral in prehistoric times.

This Sed feast chapel is the first building identified as such; and it provides a suggestive parallel to the frequent occurrence of two pyramids or tombs for a king. Seneferu had two pyramids, Unas had a pyramid and the Mastabat el Faraun, Senusert III had the north brick pyramid at Dahshur in which there is no sign of his burial, and the great sepulchre at Abydos with a granite sarcophagus very skilfully concealed. In these, and other instances, we seem to have the Sed cenotaph and worship of the king, besides his actual burial in another place.

At about a hundred yards behind the chapel, on the flat top of the hill, there stood another block of building, of which the plan is shewn on Pl. VIII. The entrance was on the south side; the two halls, south and north, had each eight columns. As the stone bases are only 19 inches across, it is probable that the columns were of wood. The fact that the columns do not divide the breadth equally, suggests that the space between them was not roofed, but each hall was an atrium open to the sky between the columns. Between the halls there were three chambers, of which the easternmost may have been all in one with the south hall. Along the north side were some benches of brickwork. On the east side of the north hall were some pieces of rough wood and some grass fibre, which seemed to have been parts of bed-frames. About a foot of the walls remains in most parts, varying from an inch or two to a couple of feet.

There is no satisfactory relation of the dimensions of the chapel and the halls. It seems that a cubit of 20·6 inches may have been used in the chapel, and of 21·0 inches in the halls.

CHAPTER III

THE INTACT BURIAL OF THE XVIIth DYNASTY.

12. AFTER trenching closely over much of the sides of the first valley to the north of the road to the Tombs of the Kings, I noticed a projecting face of rock in a retired branch of the valley. This is marked on the plan (Pl. IV), at a little above the zero of the scales, by the letter B. In the ground below this were several natural boulders lying close together. When our men came to clear amongst these they found that they covered a burial, which was placed in an open shallow trench in the rock. The plan of the group is shewn in Pl. XXII. The head was to the west, and the rock scarp overhung the basket side of the group on the south. The rock trench held the coffin and the objects at the sides of it; but the minor coffin, on and beyond the feet, was above the rock cutting. The photographs of the objects in position will shew the general arrangement, Pls. XXIII, XXIV.

13. Beginning on the outer side of the group there was a stick roughly trimmed at the knots, but with the bark on, 50·8 inches long. Upon this ten nets had been slung containing pottery. At the east end were three nets, each containing two pans of thin polished red pottery with black tops (Pl. XXVIII). Next was a long jar in a knotted string bag (Pl. XXVIII), then a long jar in an open net-work (Pl. XXVII). A bare interval on the stick shewed the space where it had been carried on the shoulder. Then came two small pots with the netting much decayed. After two long jars in the ground came a pot turned mouth down, with good netting, another hanging with netting decayed, and a drab pot in netting which had slipped off the end of the stick. All of the nettings were in a very tender state, and only the string bag would bear handling. The gravel was carefully picked away, the dust blown off while holding the net down, and then collodion was dropped over the threads to consolidate them. The entire clearance of this burial occupied about five hours, though in ordinary antiquity digging it would have been rifled in ten minutes. The main part of the interest consisted in these very rare net-works, which

could not be handled without careful preparation on the spot, and would otherwise have perished.

14. Thrust down between the coffin and the rock was the chair (Pl. XXVI.) with the upper side next to the coffin. The four legs were broken off, and thrust down the side of the coffin further to the east. It is evident that the breaking was done violently, at the burial. The chair seat is square, and accurately made, the sides being 17˙48, 17˙44, 17˙47, 17˙57 inches, average 17˙49, evidently the short cubit. This is not the cubit of 6/7 of the royal cubit, but of 24 true digits, of ˙729 inch. The height is also even, being 9˙96, 10˙00, 10˙01 and 10˙06 inches, average 10˙01. The threading is continuous, passing through 18 holes in each side; 18 threads go through each hole, three bands of three threads each running off to the two diagonals. Each band of three threads passes under three other bands, and then over three, to form the pattern. The legs are stiffened sideways by long angle pieces, or knees, cut out of natural branching of wood.

Between the chair seat and the coffin was a little bowl dropped in on edge, and a pan on edge against the shoulder beyond the chair. These were each full of dried grapes and dates (Pl. XXV). Below the pan were also pieces of bread, shewn in the photograph, and some *dūm* nuts, larger than usual, 3˙1, 2˙6, 2˙6 inches long. The larger one has the marks of three teeth in it. At the foot of the small coffin stood an upright jar.

On the south, or further side, were two stool frames, still jointed, but without any of the webbing across. Two turns of webbing left on one side of the larger stool shews it to have been twisted rush; and it seems to have entirely decayed otherwise. The larger, eastern, stool (Pl. XXVI) is 12½ × 12 inches over all, and 5½ high; it had been much used, as the rush twist had deeply ground into the wood, shewing ten lines to the inch. The smaller stool (Pl. XXVI) is 11 × 10 inches over all, and 4 high. It shews no sign of wear from webbing, and as scraps of linen cloth stuck to one side, it was probably seated with linen. The feet are not at all worn; whereas those of the larger stool are ground down with use, and chips dragged off each foot.

Below the small stool, jammed against the coffin foot, was a box (Pl. XXVI), upside down. It is 15˙2 × 7˙3 × 5˙9 inches high. The lid draws off in dovetail grooves in the usual way; on the end of this lid is a peg, to be lashed to another peg on the box-end, for sealing it up. Inside it is 13˙5 × 5˙5 to

5˙9 inches. It had contained a large lump of fatty matter, and some clothing pressed in over it. The fat, or ointment, has now soaked into the linen.

15. Next to that was a basket (Pl. XXVI), originally 10 inches across, but now pressed oval; it is 4˙8 deep and the lid is 9˙0 inches across. The lid was laid in upside down. In it was a horn, a blue marble bowl with monkeys, a bronze cutter, a sharpening stone, two flints and a ball of thread. The horn (Pl. XXV) has the end covered with a plate of ivory which is cemented on, and it therefore was permanently closed. The 8 rays of the pattern are inlaid with slips of ebony, five of which remain. The point has a ring of ivory round it, and upon the end is a bird's head with a spout carved at the top of it. The bird's beak was of black horn, now partly decayed. The neck of the bird was anciently cracked, and has been bound round with a strip of red leather.

The blue marble bowl (Pl. XXV) is 4˙8 inches across over all, the mouth 3˙8. It has four monkeys around it with outstretched arms. Their tails together form the circle of the base. The marble has a strong fluorescent blue hue inside. The bronze cutter is for cutting out linen, 5˙9 inches long. The type is more developed than that of the XIIth dynasty, but not quite so advanced as in the XVIIIth. The sharpening stone is 2˙4 long, and ˙9 inch wide at the base. The flint flakes do not look used, and are only roughly struck, and not shaped. The ball of thread is 1½ inches diameter.

Beyond the basket were two small pottery vases (Pl. XXVII), tied down over the tops, and linked together with thread. Behind these was a small upright vase, also of polished red pottery. Near the shoulder was a rough pottery jar standing upright (Pl. XXII).

16. The coffin (Pl. XXIII) is cut out of a single block of wood, and the lid is likewise a single block. The wig is of blue with goldfoil stripes; the forehead, face and breast, goldfoil; the wings, blue feathers with black lines, and gold stripes between. The length over all is 81 inches. Down the middle a formula is stamped by a wooden mould upon the gilded stucco, but no name has been inserted. On the foot end are kneeling figures of Isis and Nebhat mourning.

Inside the coffin lay the mummy, with two large shrouds spread over the whole; each shroud doubled, and then tucked in all round the edge. On removing these, and a bag of bran which lay between them down the right side, the mummy was seen swathed round spirally with nine turns of cloth from end to end, and with loose blue beads scattered over it. At the right side of the head was an alabaster jar (Pl. XXVII lower) in the corner, resting on the end of a head-rest (Pl. XXV). The head-rest is 12·25 inches long at the base, 6·90 at the top. Its stem is octagonal, each side inlaid with three squares, of ebony and ivory divided diagonally. Lying partly on the head-rest and hanging down the alabaster jar was a bead net-work pouch with handles, as in Pl. XXV. Further down the head at the shoulder was a small basket tied up (Pl. XXVI), and inside it was an alabaster kohl pot tied over with cloth, and the kohl stick put through the tie (Pl. XXVII upper). Near the feet on the left side was a smaller kohl pot of obsidian (Pl. XXV). Beneath the neck was a thin red and black pottery pan (Pl. XXVIII) lying on its side.

Beneath the head lay a second bead pouch with handles and a tassel below (Pl. XXV); both these pouches are of small blue beads. Also 16 strings of long blue beads, 8 inches long, united in a twisted thread handle, apparently a fly whisk (Pl. XXV).

17. The mummy was unwrapped by me, and with the aid of our party of five a record was kept of each separate cloth. The dimensions of the cloths, and of the warp and woof, are here given after the description. Beginning at the outside there was—

(1) At the feet a roll of very coarse linen with a fringe on the inner end of the piece. Selvedged on each side.

(2) Remains of ties around the body, made of a tube of linen sewn up; one tube 8 inches, the other 10 inches around, hemmed at ends.

(3) Shroud folded in two, laid over the body and tucked in around. One selvedge.

(4) Shroud, similarly placed. One selvedge, one end hemmed.

(5) Swathing-cloth, spread over head, and then hanked nine times round the body, seven turns downward and two upward from the feet. No selvedges. Seen in Pl. XXIII.

(6) Cloth under body; edges turned up and lapped one over the other. Folded in four across. One selvedge, one end hemmed.

(7) Cloth under body; edges turned up roughly. Folded in two across. Selvedge one side, and one end; other end with three stout threads together near rough end.

(8) Cloth, folded in two across, laid under body, edges roughly turned up, much grease on it. One selvedge, one end hemmed.

(9) Cloth, folded across in eight, laid under body with edges roughly turned over; grease on it. One selvedge, one edge woven-in fringe.

(10) Cloth, folded in two along middle lengthways, swathed diagonally round the body. Selvedge end and side.

(11) Cloth doubled across, under body, edges turned up over. One selvedge side and end.

(12) Similar to 11.

(13) Cloth folded lengthways in two, swathed diagonally round the body. One selvedge.

(14) Cloth folded in two across, laid under body edges folded up, and end tucked up over feet One side and end selvedge.

(15) Cloth laid under body, and ends turned up. Too much rotted to measure.

Inside all, the legs were wrapped separately, and the arms, hands, and fingers each wrapped diagonally separately. Pads of small cloths were used, but the whole was so much rotted by insects and decay, and loosened by the decay of all the flesh and shifting of bones, that the exact position could not be seen. Inside the stomach and pelvis was a thick mass of cloth squeezed in tightly, taking a mould of the whole hollow, 10 inches long, 7½ wide, 2½ thick. A large quantity of dark brown dust lay around the bones. The whole skeleton was perfectly preserved, the bones hard and greasy.

The cloths described above measure as follows :—

		Inches.		Threads in inches.	
		Long.	Wide.	Warp.	Woof.
(1)		115	14	21	15
(2)	{ 60	8		70	38
	{ 105	10			
(3)		176	57	128	56
(4)		171	58	92	38
(5)		189	29	86	62
(6)		328	51	54	27
(7)		164	50	62	35
(8)		166	52	76	40
(9)		711	60	76	40
(10)		141	56	42	25
(11)		164	53	70	62
(12)		170	58	138	40
(13)		283	52	49	32
(14)		182	51	62	38
(15)		rotted		50	35

From these measures we can see that cloths 7 and 14 are probably of one piece, 8 and 9 are of one piece, and 13 and 15 also of one piece. The lengths are even numbers of cubits in many cases; 105 ÷ 5; 164, 164, 166 ÷ 8; 328 ÷ 16; shewing a cubit of 20½ to 21 inches. The breadths of 50 to 53 inches which are frequent seem to be 2½ cubits. But it is strange that there is only a single wrapping-cloth with selvedges on both sides; all of the others seem to have been reduced by tearing off an edge.

The whole system of the wrapping, from in outwards, seems to have been, swathing of fingers and limbs, two folded-up cloths, a diagonal swathing, two more folded-up cloths, a diagonal swathing, four folded-up cloths, a diagonal swathing, and two loose shrouds over all. There was no sewing up, or neat packing or folding, at any part.

18. Upon the body was a green scarab, with *nofer* in scrolls, tied by string on to the third finger of the left hand. For this and all the jewellery see Pl. XXIX. On each arm, just below the elbow joint, were two plain gold bangles, oval, 2·30 and 2·44 inches wide. Around the waist, outside the innermost cloth, was a girdle of electrum beads, 26 of semicircular form, copied from a disc of leather folded over and stitched; the spaces between these had two threads of six beads each, and in one case a space of seven beads. Three spaces had been gathered together by a tie of thread, so as to shorten the circuit of the girdle to fit the body. The whole girdle was 31·6 inches long, and was shortened to 28·4. Loose about the head were two gold ear-rings or hair-rings, ·90 across and ·36 inch wide. The four component rings are each made hollow, but not so thin as the later ear-rings of the XVIIIth dynasty.

On the neck was a collar of four rows of small rings of gold. These rings are ·17 inch diameter; and thick enough not to collapse when squeezed between the fingers. They are flat on the inside, but rounded or bevelled on the outside. Each has been soldered to join it. The four strings are—

13·1 inches long of 394 rings
14·0   ,,   ,,   ,, 416 ,,
14·7   ,,   ,,   ,, 422 ,,
15·2   ,,   ,,   ,, 421 ,,

varying from 27½ to 30 to the inch, and widening downwards on the slope of the neck. Besides these there is ·63 inch width of the junction piece. The junction piece is made of two similar halves. Each half has four tubes for the ends of the threads Each tube is made by soldering eight rings together. At the junction ends each tube has a hemispherical cup soldered on to it. Inside each hemisphere is soldered a ring of wire. When the two halves are put together the rings alternate in one line, and are held in unison by a gold pin dropping through all the eight rings. The pin tapers from ·04 to ·02 near the point; the head is ·08 wide; the length is ·80 inch. When found, the pin had been put in from below upward by the undertaker; but this was wrong, as it will only go home in the reverse direction. Each of the hemispheres which close the tubes is pierced, doubtless for the master-thread of the stringing to pass through, and be knotted to secure it. A very thick pack of fibre filled the rings; so compact that only two rings could be dragged off at a time, and then the fibre had to be sliced off close before withdrawing more. The fibre was too much rotted to be retained, as the collar could not be straightened or cleaned without its breaking short. The whole was therefore restrung, keeping the original order of the rings.

On the neck of the inner garment was an electrum button. The disc of it is oval, ·50 × ·37 inch, and very thin. The shank is pointed like a nail; ·28 long and ·06 inch thick. The edge of the garment was attached to this shank by a cord of threads lashed on to it. It is remarkable that a ring shank was not used, such as is found in the Ist dynasty jewellery, and the VIth dynasty buttons. This looks rather as if it had been an ornamental nail, for decorating woodwork, made to serve for a button.

The weights of the various parts are—

		Grains.
Bangles . . 322·7, 324·4, 325·6, 325·8 =		1298·5
Girdle		352?
Ear-rings . . . 133·8, 138·8 =		272·6
Strings of rings . 349·4, 364·9, 394·0, 392·6 }		
Connecting piece of collar . 39·8, 41·4, 3·2 } =		1585·4
Button		11·7
Total		3520·

From the near equality of the bangles it appears that they were carefully weighed. But their weights do not conform to any standard except the 80-grain. This is believed to have been derived from repeated halving of the Assyrian "stone" of 10 shekels, and the total of the 4 bangles is 10 shekels. The bangles then are 4 of 80-grain unit; the collar is 20 of the unit, and the junction piece is half a unit on each side. The unit varies from 79·3 to 81·5 grains here, and its general limits are 79 to 81 grains. As it was a Syrian unit, it was probably of Hyksos importation in the XVIIth dynasty.

19. The skeleton was in excellent condition, that of a woman in the prime of life. The teeth were but little worn; they are rather projecting, though the face is not prognathous in structure. The arms were down the sides, and the hands on the front of the thighs. The dimensions of the skull were, in millimetres, length 167; breadth max. 132, bizygomatic 121, biauricular 110; height 127; basi-nasal 95, basi-alveolar 92, nasi-alveolar 68; nasal height 49, breadth 23; facial height (nasion to chin) 111; jaw height (to meeting of teeth) 38; jaw length 109; jaw breadth at base 88, at hinge 107. Humeri, R. 289, L. 296. Ulnae, R. 249, L. 248. Femora 412, both. Tibiae, R. 339, L. 338. As compared with average women of the XIth dynasty, the head is short, rather low, but a fair width; the mouth is low in the face; the nose long and narrow, and the jaw rather small in front view. On the whole it is a high type of face, except for the projection and size of the teeth.

As regards the date of the burial, the red polished pottery is most like that of the early XVIIIth dynasty, and cannot be placed anywhere near the XIIth. The diagonal pattern of inlay on the head-rest is like that on the bead bracelets of Aah-hotep, and the girdle beads like hers, at the end of the XVIIth dynasty. The bronze cutter is later than the XIIth, but not quite as developed as that of the XVIIIth dynasty. The blue marble bowl is like the work of the XIIth; but the kohl pots have the high shoulder of the XVIIIth dynasty. On the whole it might well be placed in the XVIIth dynasty.

20. The burial of an infant was in a box (Pl. XXVI), plain whitewashed, 37·6 inches long, 12 wide, 9½ deep over all. The skull was all but closed at the top, and hence it was not new-born. Over the whole was a cloth 130 × 46 inches, folded to a quarter of the length, and half the breadth, 32 × 23, and tucked in at the sides of the body. Next a cloth 172 × 54, much folded in length and creased to fit the width of the box, and the 54-inch width went over the length of the body, and was tucked in under the head. Then the body was wrapped in about a dozen turns of cloth, but so much decayed and eaten and stuck together that it could not be separated. The limbs were wrapped separately, the

arms were down the sides. On the neck was a thread of 215 small gold ring-beads ·05 inch diameter, 42 to the inch; they are only coiled and not soldered. At the right ear was a spoiled group of 3½ gold rings stuck together, looking like a miniature ear-ring, and a similar group at the left. It is evident that some rings like the ring-beads of the woman's necklace but rather larger (·25 wide), had been over-heated while on a mandril in the furnace for soldering; the solder had stuck them together, and they parted and began to drop away, being half melted. On the left humerus were two ivory bangles, 1¾ inch inside width, 2¼ outside, and ·15 thick. On the right humerus was one bangle, 1¾ inside, 2 outside width, and ·17 thick. Round the waist was a string of small blue ring-beads 19½ inches long, and round each ankle a string of similar beads.

Though this burial was only in the open ground yet it is very complete in personal objects. Probably it is the richest and most detailed undisturbed burial that has been completely recorded and published.

CHAPTER IV

THE PAINTED TOMBS, XVIITH—XXTH DYNASTIES.

21. THE earliest painted tomb that we met with was in a very large rock-pit in the mouth of the small valley at the north end of Drah abul Nega. This pit was about twenty feet square, and had been painted. Only a small part of the fresco remained, on the north side, which is here published as a frontispiece. It had been excavated by some one in recent years. As it was impossible to preserve the fragment of painted wall by any door or reasonable cage over it, I was authorised to remove it, which I did in sections. The work is closely like that of the Isis and Nebhat figures on the foot of the XVIIth dynasty coffin, and it is probably of that age.

The large rock-chamber had originally been self-roofed; but the top had nearly all fallen in. The original entrance was by a brick tunnel about thirty feet long; and, though both ends of the tunnel were broken, there was some probability that the objects in it had been taken out of the tomb when originally plundered. They are all given in Pl. XXXI, 8-15. The cone, 13, is of the hereditary prince, keeper of the temple of Mentu in Erment, named Senmut. This was of course not the celebrated Senmut the architect of Hatshepsut. The kohl vases of black serpentine, 12, 14, have the sharp shoulder of the XVIIth—XVIIIth dynasties. The fragments of steles, 9, 10, are very rough in lettering, and show that this cannot be dated to the XVIIIth dynasty. The kneeling figure, 11, which originally held a tablet, is of good work, like those of the early XVIIIth dynasty. The bowl, 15, is of the same age.

The fresco (frontispiece) which remained was on the north wall of the chamber, to the west of the door; there were also a few traces of figures to the east of the door. The rock had been roughly flattened, then coated with a layer of mud and straw, and the face of that whitewashed. Upon the yellow-white face the figures were drawn with black for the outlines and hair, yellow for the flesh, white for the dress, and occasionally some red. The top line shows a row of singers beating time with their hands; the name is placed to one of them, Se-ankh-nu. In the second line the women are dancing and snapping their fingers. In the third line is a larger figure, which seems to have been a principal servant with offerings, "made by her praiser Sit-hathor." The dancers are as above, superintended by two men, Uazy and Mery. In the base line are pairs of women holding each other by the hand, probably engaged in a slow dance, as the heel of one is raised from the ground. This is one of the few remains that we have of the rough but spirited archaic work which preceded the rise of the art of the XVIIIth dynasty.

22. An interesting small tomb at the north end of Drah abul Nega belonged to a man Baka and his wife Mes. It is situated in the plain, at the extreme N.E. foot of the hill, facing on the road which skirts the bottom of the slope. It belongs probably to the age of Tahutmes I, as the keeper of the cattle of the deceased queen Aahmes Nefertari is named. The scenes show some good details, though much injured, like other open tombs. My wife copied the less usual subjects, which are here reproduced on Pls. XXXIV to XXXVII.

Pl. XXXIV. A figure of the son of the family, Auab, standing. Behind him is a girl playing double pipes, and another clapping her hands. Above them are jars placed in stands, which may be compared with *Gizeh and Rifeh*, Pl. XXVII E, 82.

Pl. XXXV shows two scenes of weighing. In the upper one the weigher is steadying the plumb-bob of the balance to see if it is exact, while the scribe is recording the amount. The stand before the balance has on it weights of a dome form, and in the shape of a hippopotamus. Compare with this the weight in the form of a hippopotamus head found at Nubt (*Naqada*, p. 67). Below this is another scene, of weighing metal vases, and one of the weights in the scale is in the form of a calf; this form is known on monuments and in actual examples.

Pl. XXXVI. At the top is a scene of storing wine in jars. Below are figures of men who are hauling at a clap-net, while another man seated is cleaning the ducks that were caught, and hanging them up ready for cooking.

Pl. XXXVII gives three separate pieces. A fine goose shews detail of colouring. A beautiful figure of the sister of Baka, named Taro, shews her seated on the ground smelling a lotus. Below is a scene of wildfowl over a thicket of papyri.

23. The tomb of Amen-mes is toward the northern end of Drah abul Nega, and the connections of it are described at the beginning of the next chapter. It was painted about the time of Amenhotep II; and, though greatly destroyed, it yet contains many fragments of scenes which show that it was of the best work of that age. A few details are given on Pl. XXXVIII. The cylindrical jars used in offering, or placed in stands, are of forms well known at that age. But the "salad-mixer" type of vase in a stand, with papyri between, is fresh to us at this period, and the cups on stands below that are also unusual. The two figures of the tomb front give details of the column, like those of Tell el Amarna tombs, and of the funeral stele placed in a niche in the pyramidion upon the tomb. This latter shows the origin of the so-called window niche in the top of the Meroitic pyramids.

24. Opposite to the tomb of Amen-mes, in the same court, is a later tomb of the keeper of the cattle of Amen in Thebes, Piaay. This is probably of the XXth dynasty, and the colouring is flat and poor. Two parts were selected for copying, here given on Pl. XXXIX. The first scene on the right is of carrying the shrine of Horus in procession, with fans of feathers, and offering incense before it. On the left is the figure of Osiris enthroned, with Isis and Nebhat behind him and the four genii in front of him. Horus comes before him to introduce Piaay (continued in lower line), who is bowing before the god. Next is the scene of weighing the heart, with Piaay and his wife bowing before the weighers. Above this were alternations of the head of Hathor and the name and titles of Piaay.

CHAPTER V

THE XVIIITH AND XIXTH DYNASTIES.

25. THE most important objects of the XVIIIth dynasty were figures found in a tomb pit, anciently plundered, towards the north end of Drah abul Nega. This pit was in a small court, which had the tomb of Amen-mes on the south, that of Piaay standing open on the north, and a plain passage tomb on the west. In the north side of the floor was a small unopened pit and chamber with two burials of the XXVth dynasty, described in the next chapter; and in the north-west corner was a deep tomb pit for which the open court had probably been originally made. In this tomb pit was a seated black granite figure, broken in two pieces and some fragments (Pl. XXXII), and the upper part of a figure in limestone (Pl. XXXIII). The granite figure is of the scribe of the accounts of corn in the southern cities, Usi, son of Si-amen. It is as good as any granite work of the New Kingdom. The limestone figure is of the finest work of that age, with the suavity and beauty which characterise it. Unfortunately it does not bear any inscription.

26. Beneath the temple of Nebunnef the earlier tombs had scarcely been touched in modern times; we were therefore able to obtain some steles, pottery, and other objects. The earliest object is a limestone figure, seated cross-legged, of the king's son Antef-mes, called Mes-tesher, the "red child" (XXX, 3). It is decayed by the damp, but interesting from its age. A fragment, XXX, 4, appears to be of a stele of one of the Antefs, Ra-seshes-her-maat or Ra-seshes-up-maat, adoring Amen. A stele of a man and his wife, XXX, 1, appears to be of about the XVIIth dynasty. Half of a black granite base, XXX, 2, was made for the figures of the keeper of the granary of Amen, Setu, and his sister Usi. A piece of limestone with large fine hieroglyphs in relief, XXX, 7, was found in the ruins of the Nebunnef temple; it seems to be part of a tomb of a scribe of accounts. The piece of a black granite sarcophagus, XXX, 5, was bought; it is of the celebrated architect Amenhotep, son of Hapu, whose tomb is as yet unknown. Pieces of steles were also found in the temple of Nebunnef, of Huy, a scribe of Amen, XII, 22; of King Amenhotep I, XII, 23, singularly like Tahutmes III in features; and of a priest Huy adoring Amenhotep and Aahmes Nefer-tari, XII, 24.

There are also some tomb objects from the same burial place. The couch and figure of red pottery, XXXI, 5, throw some light on the frequent female figures found in tombs. It has been supposed that they were votive after childbirth, or to represent a wife for the deceased, sometimes with a child. The latter motive is shown here by the couch having a double pillow, but only one figure to lay upon it. These female figures were therefore intended for the benefit of the deceased like the pottery soul-houses, furniture, and food offerings. Probably the so-called dolls, XX, 607, XXXI, 6, 7, were likewise wives. A stone head-rest was found with pottery in another tomb, XX, 604. A brown serpentine vase, XL, 656, was with pottery of the XVIIIth dynasty. And a flask of the black pottery, descended from the prick pattern pottery of Hyksos times, was of the same age, XL, 648. The pottery box-coffin, XL, 654, was in a grave with cones of Khauiy. Similar graves were found under the store-rooms of Sety I. In one of these was a group of hollow silver bangles, much corroded, an alabaster cup, a green paste bowl, and kohl pots of black serpentine and alabaster, XXXI, 16-20. In another grave was a black limestone kohl pot with haematite stick, two cutting-out knives, two needles, and pieces of pyrites and blue glass, XXXI, 22-9.

Pottery cones were often found; those of ten different persons were built into the brick covering over the tomb of the XXVth dynasty, and thirteen others were found in the tombs under the temple of Nebunnef. The names upon these will be published next year, as further work is intended at Qurneh, and more may be discovered.

27. The pottery of the XVIIIth dynasty is shown on Pls. XLI, XLII. The tube pots 678-89 are of the earlier part of the dynasty, as shown by the dating at Rifeh. The blue colouring on 690 shows that it is of Amenhotep II or later. The screw-top pattern 691-2 is of Tahutmes I or earlier, see *Gizeh and Rifeh*, XXVII E, 90, 91. The forms 693-4 are of Tahutmes III, see *Rifeh* 209. No. 696 is probably earlier, see *Rifeh* 190, 192. The succeeding forms to 704 are of Tahutmes III, or a little later, see *Rifeh* 254-5, 325, 349-51. The black bands and red and black 705-10 are also of Tahutmes III, see *Rifeh* 248-50. The well-formed oval bottles 720-6 are of Tahutmes III (*Rifeh* 269), while the angular high-shoulders, as 711-16, are later (*Rifeh* 383, 386). The coarse jars 728-30 are probably of the XIXth dynasty.

We now note some groups of pottery found in

tombs under the Nebunnef temple, N 4, N8. The small pot 735 was found with the alabaster kohl pot 736. The variety of form of 744–57 is puzzling. Some, as 749, 750, seem clearly of middle XVIIIth dynasty (*Rifeh* 383); also compare 751 with *Rifeh* 313, and 747–8 with *Rifeh* 166. Yet the dull pinky-brown colour and forms of 753–6 seem almost as if Ptolemaic. The same grouping is however found in another tomb where 741 was along with the cup 746. Then again 757 looks certainly like much later pottery, being an almost globular pilgrim bottle of large size, like 742, 743 (not in groups); only as the pilgrim bottle begins in the XVIIIth dynasty, it is possible that large sizes were then made. We must hesitate then where to date 741, 753–6, which seem to be foreign pottery, and for which the XVIIIth dynasty is indicated. The two red polished jars 737, 738, the latter with black top, seem also to be foreign, perhaps Nubian. The tomb B 15 in which they were found was of the XIth dynasty.

28. In the temple of Sety I at Qurneh a few of the most important parts were copied facsimile in full size. In Pl. XLIII is the figure of Rameses I in his shrine, protected by the hawk above it; this is from chamber F of Baedeker's plan. The hawk is entitled " Horus the son of Osiris protecting the king Rameses." And before the king is " The Osiris the king Men-pehti-ra *ma-kheru* Rameses *ma-kheru*." The strip of inscription is that down the jambs of the door of the chamber containing the shrine scene, recording "the son of the sun, lord of the crowns, Mery Amen Rameses, made by him for his monuments for the father of his father the good god Men-pehti-ra *ma-kheru*." This inscription was therefore set up by Rameses II.

Pl. XLIV shews the row of standards on the sides of the central chamber; parts defective on one side have been completed here from the opposite scene. These appear to be the standards of the principal centres of early Egyptian worship. The ram is Khnumu of the Ist nome, Elephantine. The next is the head of Mut of the IVth nome, Thebes. Next come the two hawks of the Vth nome, Koptos. Then the sacred head or wig of Osiris of the VIIIth nome, Abydos. Following are the jackals, Upuati of the south and of the north, of the XIIIth nome, Asyut. Then a king's head which may be that of the XXth nome, Henen-suten, or the royal youth. The sistrum may be that of Hathor of the XXIInd nome, Aphroditopolis. Lastly is the mace of Memphis, the name of which city, *Anbu hez*, may more

likely mean the fortification of the mace-bearing king, rather than merely the "white wall." The mace is here upheld by a support, like that shewn upholding the statues of Min.

Pl. XLV. At the top is the head of the *ka* of the temple, with the name of the " Divine House of the son of the sun Sety Merenptah in the dwelling of Amen on the west of Thebes." Beside it is a copy of the tablet of Siptah, adoring Aahmes Nefertari, Sety I, and Ramessu II, inscribed on the front wall north of the entrance. This was also at one time inscribed by Amen-messu; and it has been published by Lepsius (*Denk.* iii, 201 *c*) in so conventional a style that it is desirable to shew the actual appearance of it, which is very rude. There are a few differences between the readings here and those of Lepsius; in some of these the present reading is certainly right, the others must be examined in future. But as evidently the later conditions of lighting were better than those for the earlier copy, the present readings must be considered. Below is a group of offerings, to shew the forms of the various vases. The strange rectangles on stands at the right hand are very unusual.

29. While waiting for permission to extend our work to the Nebunnef site I worked over a part of the store-chambers of the temple of Sety I. Most of the pottery belonged to later occupation down to the XXVIth dynasty. Below it were many sealings of coarse plaster, from which I copied sixteen different seals, given in Pl. XLVI. Seals 1 and 2 are for "Oil of the glorious temple of Sety in the house of Amen." Seal 3 is for "Wine of the glorious temple of Sety." Seal 4 for " Wine of the glorious temple of Sety in the house of Amen." Seal 5, "Wine of the (glorious) temple of Sety." Seal 6 only reads " Wine of Sety. . . ." Seal 7 is " Men-maat-ra oil of. . . ." Seal 8 reads " Palace of Maat-men-ra, excellent wine from upon the west (of Thebes)." Seal 9 is " Men-maat-ra, unguent of the palace upon the west of Thebes." Seal 10, " Men-maat-ra, honey of the palace upon the west of Thebes." Seal 11 is for "Wine of . . . of Uti." Seal 12 is remarkable, being for " Oil of the house of Bantanta," shewing that oil was still brought to this temple late in the reign of Ramessu II, after his daughter had estates. Seal 13 is for " Fresh oil of ducks " or animal oil. Seal 14 may have had a ram's head with the double feather. Seals 15, 16 are a well-known type, " Arat nefer (neb) ka," or the *ka* of the good goddess, or of Uazet. No. 17 is a stamp of the palace of Ramessu Meri-

amen. No. 18 is a fragment of the name and titles of Nebunnef from his temple.

30. As soon as Prof. Maspero agreed to my working further on the edge of the desert, I began upon a site between the temple of Amenhotep I and that of Sety I. There lay on the surface two broken colossi of black granite, with the names of Ramessu II, and some blocks of stone were visible in the ground. We began to clear the site along the east side, and advanced across to the west. The blocks found here were none of them above the floor-level of the temple; they consisted of foundations, mostly level with the floor, as shewn by the bases of two columns. The plan given in Pl. XLVII was made by laying out lines of taping at 200 inches apart, the line of zeros being square with the taped lines. Offsets were then measured to points of each stone, and drawn on squared paper one by one as they were measured.

Beginning at the south end, there are the two colossi, which are here shaded with cross-lines, the foot end of the base being separated by a line. The shading does not shew the present places of the blocks, but the positions where they last stood before they were tilted over to be broken up. They seem to have been placed upon the blocks of stone north of them, and to have been dragged forward and twisted round before they were broken up. The estimated positions of columns and walls are shewn by dotted lines. The row of columns on the western side of the peristyle court was curiously askew, and the axis from between the bases of the colossi to the temple behind is similarly askew, as well as the west boundary-wall of brick. The cause of this is not known. Another strange irregularity is having three intercolumniations on the west of the temple door, and only two on the east side. The diameters of the column bases drawn here were fixed by finding half of the base in the middle of the east side, 56 inches across.

From the row of small blocks, and the width of interval between the southern columns and the front wall of the temple, it seems as if there were two rows of columns on the north side of the court. The front wall of the temple is defined by the line of blocks, and by one at the entrance to the west chamber being a door-sill of sandstone among all the other blocks of limestone. The chambers on the east must have been wider than those on the west, as shewn both by the places of the foundations and by the places of the column bases of sandstone. The cross-wall in the middle of the temple is only suggested by

a few blocks, but in any case it is not likely that chambers would have been so long as 45 feet while only 8 or 12 feet wide.

The date of the building is only given by the foundation deposits. One deposit is marked DEP.; another was at about a symmetrical position on the east (unfortunately omitted in planning); and perhaps there was an axial one in the same line, as many scattered objects were found along this region. The arrangement of the parts of the eastern deposit which remained in place is shewn on the left side of Pl. VIII. Two small boxes of brickwork each contained two limestone tablets (N) inscribed for Nebunnef, high priest of Amen and Ramessu II. For these and other objects see Pl. XXXIII. In the south box between the limestone tablets was a green glazed one (B) of Ramessu II. In the south-east corners of the boxes were corn-grinders of limestone (L) and granite (GR). The small glazed objects had all been scattered at the upheaval of the limestone foundations. The colours of them were blue 157 objects, red 39, white 15, brown-black 13. Of the royal plaques of Ramessu II most were with the *user* on legs, or *se-user* a form rarely found, and apparently by this preceding the usual form. The total numbers of objects found are—

Cartouches, *Seuser-maat-ra*	.	.	.	12
User-maat-ra	.	.	.	1
Ramessu	.	.	.	9
Nebunnef, high priest of Amen	.	.	5
Ox with legs bound	.	.	.	32
Ox haunch	.	.	.	72
Ox head	.	.	.	45
Bunch of vegetables (?)	.	.	.	24
Grain of corn	.	.	.	24
				——
				224

There were also one each of bronze models of axe, adze, knife, borer, and lever. The limestone block in the western deposit names Nebunnef as high priest of Hathor. In his tomb at Thebes is an inscription naming the first year of Ramessu II, which shews that he was high priest at the king's accession. He seems to have built this temple as a small work of his own while directing the adjacent temple building of Sety I at Qurneh; and he was somewhat independent under the new king, as he put his own name and titles on the foundation tablets.

31. In a tomb high up on the southern side of the little valley, at the north end of Drah abul Nega,

the wall is squared for drawing figures. These squared drawings are shewn on Pl. XLVIII. The figure is 19¼ squares in height. The size of squares is 2·374 inches each for the larger figure, and 2·376 horizontally and 2·330 vertically for the smaller figure. This size does not seem to belong to any usual standard; it may be a sixth of a cubit of 20 digits of ·713 inch. In another tomb near by are squares of ·5864 inch, evidently fifths of a palm, shewing a digit of ·733 inch, or cubit of 20·52 inches. The same size of squares occurs on a draughtsman's slab at Memphis. Another scene in the same tomb has squares of ·717 inch, a very short digit.

CHAPTER VI

THE LATER PERIODS.

32. POTTERY of about the XXIInd dynasty was found, both in the store-rooms of Sety I, and also in secondary burials in cemetery B. It is here arranged on three plates XLIX, L, LI. The bowls differ from the earlier forms in having a brim, and generally the point of the bottom deeper than the foot. They also have handles, in one case four (No 768). The lumpy drab pottery with lines around it (770–9) is only found in this period. The large jars, 780–4, are of the same greenish-grey colour; it was evidently a weak clay when wet, as shewn by the constant use of cords round it for drying. The pattern on 782 was scored on it while soft; so also was the mark on 783, which is put on opposite sides, here copied together for comparison. The other jars are all of forms well known in this age.

33. An unopened tomb of about the XXVth dynasty was found in the courtyard in which are the tombs of Amen-mes and Piaay. A thick bank of brickwork covered the floor of the court on the west, and on cutting through this it was found to cover a small square pit. The unburnt bricks were mingled with pottery cones to stiffen the mass. These cones had belonged to ten different tombs, and as those tombs are doubtless not far off around this court the names may be of use in tracing positions in the cemetery. The pit was very shallow, only just deep enough to allow of a chamber roof under the court. And it was so narrow that the outer coffins could not be taken out with lids on; there was hardly an inch to spare in removing them. The plan of the tomb will be seen on Pl. VIII, and the outer and inner coffins and furniture on Pls. LII, LIII.

On the north side was the coffin of a man, painted black and inscribed faintly, with the body bandaged with stripes around, and two diagonal bands. In the outer coffin, and upon the inner, was a mass of leaf garlands. Inside the inner coffin was a pillow under the head, and a clay figure wrapped in cloth at the right of the head; also a lotus flower upon the stomach (Pl. LIII). The woman was a chantress of Amen named Per-en-bast. Her mummy was bandaged, with some lotus flowers on it, but covered with a thin coat of pitch. Her coffin is pitched, with yellow painted designs. The eyes and eyebrows are inlaid with glass. The topmost subject is Osiris enthroned with his family, then the bust of Sokar, then the cow of Hathor and the four genii, and four seated genii with knives at the feet. Along the sides are scenes of the late mythology, the serpent spitting poison on the headless enemies, etc. At the side and head of the man's coffin were two rough black boxes; these contained respectively 200 and 203 rough brown pottery ushabtis. The numbers are marked on the plan. At the shoulder stood a Sokar-Osiris figure of pitched wood. Upon the woman's coffin were two small boxes with 185 and 183 small clay ushabtis painted blue; also a Sokar-Osiris figure. The ushabtis were all packed in clean sand. Such filling might be thought to be accidental in some cases, but here it was in boxes placed bare upon the top of a coffin in a clear chamber. The boxes, ushabtis, and figures are shewn in Pl. LIII.

34. The inscription of Haa-ab-ra on Pl. LVI is cut on a quarried face at the south end of all the valley quarries, nearest to the Kings' valley. Further up the first quarry valley, on a pillar in a cave are sketches of Ta-urt twice over, and two hunting dogs. Also in one quarry that was worked in Roman times there are two Latin inscriptions, one congratulating T. Domitius Crispus (Pl. VIII), the other a long one of which only the name Demetrius is clear. The mode of quarrying in this Roman work differed from the old Egyptian in marking off intervals with a red line, probably showing the extent of each day's work. Thus the amounts done could be compared. These red lines clearly follow the course of work, and a slight shift of the face is visible at each. There are 13 in 112 inches on the roof, and 9 in 70 inches down the side. This shews over 8½ inches a day in horizontal work, and under 8 inches in vertical. How many men were engaged along the grooves is not visible, but there must have been about four feet length to each man. As the grooves elsewhere are 18 inches wide, to allow of the worker's

body passing, there must have been about four cubic feet of stone chipped out daily by each worker. Near by is a block not yet removed. The groove round it is from 17 to 20 inches wide, and the block is 100 by 55 inches, and about 70 high. This shews that in cutting large blocks the need of the workman passing around them obliged about as much rock to be chipped out as the volume of the block which was obtained.

35. The latest class of pottery found is that of the XXVIth dynasty (Pls. LIV, LV). The forms are mostly well known of this period and perhaps rather later. The jars 833–4 and those on Pl. LV are exactly what belong to the VIIth century B.C. at Defenneh. The forms of the jars 849–57 shew them to be Greek in origin. Moreover, there are Greek monograms cut after baking, and therefore shewing the owner's marks, see next to 850. These prove the jars to have been used by Greeks. From the quantity of Greek jars, and the marks, it appears that there was a colony of Greeks at Thebes in the VIIth century. Probably this was a small Greek garrison, like the frontier garrisons, planted by Psamtek.

In a site so long occupied as Thebes the excavator has to take what comes, and should preserve the record of the remains of all periods that may be found. The present two months' work has, how-ever, cleared up the XIth dynasty cemetery and pottery, and the contemporaneous chapel of Sankh-ka-ra; while the search for tombs in the valleys has produced the most complete burial of the XVIIth dynasty, one of the best funeral series found at Thebes. The various other discoveries are welcome additions to the main matters of research, which have fully repaid the short time spent upon them while waiting to resume the great work at Memphis.

CHAPTER VII

THE INSCRIPTIONS.

By Dr. J. H. WALKER.

36. PL. III. These two steles of the XIth dynasty form an interesting addition to the very small number of steles, which have been preserved, of this period. The hieroglyphs are coarse and rudely cut, as they are on the stele of Antef V (*Koptos*, Pl. VIII), and on the contemporary steles of Dendereh (*Dend*. XI C, XII). The hieroglyph for the letter *f* has the head separated from the body, and at the end of line 2 of the second stele, in the

King's name Antef only the head of the hieroglyph appears, the body is omitted altogether. Unfortu-nately no clear historical reference is given, whereby the position of the King *Hor-uah-ankh* can be defi-nitely fixed in the dynasty. In line 4 of the second stele, the snake and feather sign of Aphroditopolis, the 10th nome of Upper Egypt, establishes this as the Northern boundary of the Kingdom of this dynasty, the "Door of the North." It clears up the badly drawn hieroglyph, determining the Northern boundary in line 3 of the stele of *Hor-uah-ankh* in Cairo Museum (*Mon. Div.* pl. 49, and *Transactions S.B.A.* iv. p. 194, also Breasted, *Ancient Records*, I. p. 200, note *a*).

The scribe has evidently confused the writing of the towns Abydos and Elephantine. In line 4 the Southern limit of the "whole Southern country" must be Elephantine, but it is written *Abu* with the city determinative, instead of the desert determinative, whilst Abydos in line 1 is written *Ab* instead of *Abdu*.

The very common formula at the beginning of both steles, which has been translated in so many different ways—the phrase *stn dj ḥtp*—I prefer to read, "May the King give an offering table" to the deity or deities mentioned. A distinction is drawn between the *ḥetep* given to a god, and the *per-kheru* funeral feasts given to mortals. I consider therefore that the phrase means "May the King give an offer-ing" to the god, in order that the god may distribute from it funeral feasts to the deceased. When in some cases no god is mentioned, but the name of the deceased follows immediately after the formula, here apparently the deceased is regarded as a god, the Osirian one, and therefore the *ḥetep* can fitly be given to him directly.

An interesting variation occurs at the end of line 1 and beginning of line 2 in the first stele. In the majority of the inscriptions, where the individual items of the funeral feasts are specified, the meat portions are represented by the head of an ox and the head of a bird. Here there are the heads of three different animals, as well as the bird. The same three animals are represented on a stele of funeral offerings, in *Koptos*, Pl. XI, 4.

37. *Stele No.* 1. "May the King give an offer-ing table to Anubis upon his hill, he who is in his mummy wrappings the lord of *Ta-zeser* (the under-world), for funeral feasts to him (*i.e.* the deceased), consisting of thousands of cups of wine, oxen, wild fowl, gazelles (?), oryxes (?), linen bandages (*šs mnḫt*), and all good things. The prince, the confidential

friend, the superintendent of the granaries (??), the governor of the Residence, Zari, says, I was known by my lord, a great one of the palace, a man of years (*s n rnpt*??), healthy of heart. I established those who knew me not, as well as those who knew me. I did that which the great ones loved, and that which was praised by the humble people, in order that Horus might extend my life upon earth (a play on the royal *Ka* name). In the next world I went forth from my house, and entered into my tomb."

In front of Zari's wife, the inscription reads, "The sole royal favourite, priestess of Hathor, Sentmentui." In front of the leg of the chair, the first hieroglyph, the wave-line '*n*', may be for the negative, and thus the inscription may read, "May there never be a going away of anything from them." The wish apparently refers to the offerings on the table, that they may be perpetual.

Stele No. 2. "May the King give an offering table to Osiris, lord of Busiris, the chief of those who are in the West, lord of Abydos. The prince, the sole confidential friend, the governor of the Residence, the superintendent of the granaries (??), Zari, says, The Horus *Uah-ankh*, the King of Upper and Lower Egypt, the son of Ra, Antef, the creator of beauties, sent me a message, after I had fought with the house of Khety (?) in the domain of Thinis, and messages came that the prince had given me a boat, in order that there might be protection for the land of those who belong to the South, to its whole extent, Southwards (?) from Elephantine and Northwards to Aphroditopolis, because he knew my excellence. I say, I was promoted amongst the elders, I was fierce (?) of heart on the day of smiting." The end of the line seems to be confused; apparently the scribe had to condense his statement, for want of space. It may read: "For greatness came upon me, because I did excellent things, I was head of my nome, a mighty man, a prince."

The vertical line on the left gives the parentage of Zari, "born of the scribe (?) . . . superintendent (?) of the valley, Hesi, the prince and sole confidential friend."

In front of Zari. "The governor of the Residence, the superintendent of the granaries (?), Zari, the excellent one, deceased. I was one who was beloved of his city, and praised by his god."

It is highly probable that Khety is the right reading for the name in line 3, and thus refers to one of the very powerful princes of Siut, who fought for the Herakleopolitan rulers of the IXth and Xth dynasties, against the rival Theban kingdom of the XIth dynasty.

38. Pl. X. Stele from tomb B 33. "May the King give an offering table, and may Anubis give an offering table, for funeral feasts to the sole confidential friend, the superintendent of the priests of Dehuti (?) . . . beloved of mankind, at the head of his fellows. I was one who provided [a gang] of twenty individuals. I was the sealer (?) of the great fields, besides the portions of my father's property. I made provisions (?) for the temple of Amen in years of scarcity. I was the sealer (?) of the sacrificial oxen (*rhs*), paying attention, at each festival of the opening of a season, to the altar tables, as far as the opening of the year festival. I acted as herdsman in charge of the asses, and as herdsman in charge of the goats, and as herdsman in charge of . . ."

It is difficult to see what the ordinal number "the 7th" (*sfh nw*) refers to, in the last line. "The 7th superintendent in the temple (*r; pr*) of Amen" seems to be quite an impossible idea.

Stele from tomb B 45, with seated figures, below. 1. "The provider (?) (*grgw*?) of the Treasury, Herhathor, deceased." 2. "The provider (?) of the Treasury, Nenni, deceased." 3. "[The lady of] the house, Ihet abu." 4. ". . . the provider (?) of the Treasury, Neferhetep, who feeds the inhabitants of his deserts on earth every day."

39. Seated figure of black granite. Pl. XXXII. "May the King give an offering table to Tum, lord of Heliopolis, and to the cycle of the gods in Asheru, in order that they may give glory, and strength, and happiness, to the *Ka* of the unique one, the excellent one, the good one who has earned the reward of merit in Thebes, the scribe of accounts in the Southern city, the scribe Usi, deceased, born of the superintendent of the granary Siamen (his father's name), born of Ked-nefer-hemt-mut (his mother's name)."

"May the King give an offering table to Amen-Ra, King of the Gods, and to Mut, lady of Asheru, in order that they may grant the receiving of *snu*-cakes, which come forth into the presence, and milk which comes forth upon the altar table, and breezes of the North wind, as daily rations for each day, to the *Ka* of the proclaimer of truth (*gr m;'*), the man of excellent merit, the good and excellent witness, the man of good character (*nb qd*), the possessor of singleness of speech (*nb r; w'*) who deals not in double-tongued speech (*tm ir nswi*), the scribe of accounts Usi."

3

INDEX

Printed by Hazell, Watson & Viney, Ld., London and Aylesbury.

H.P.

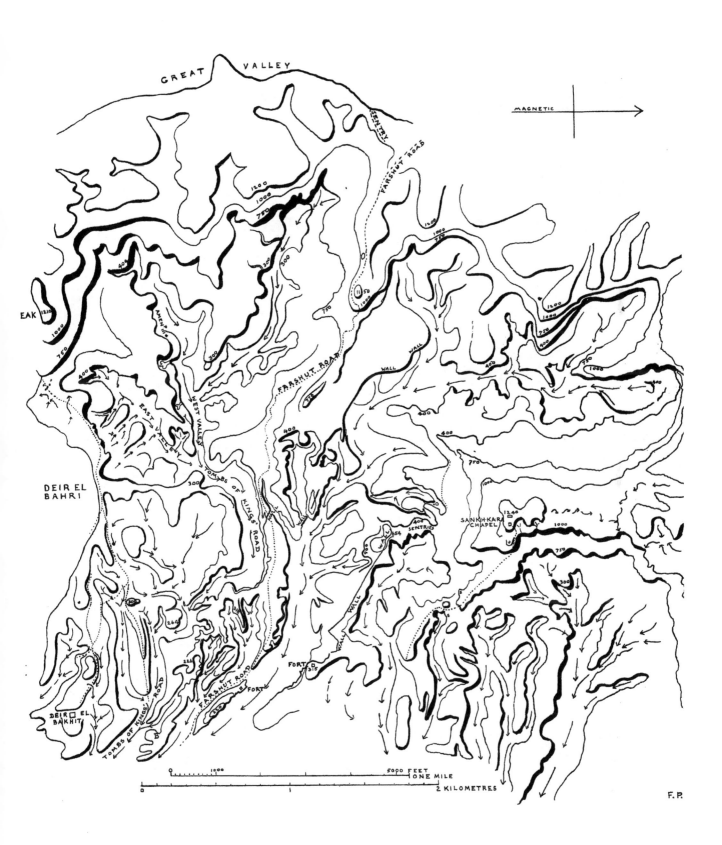

VIEW OF HILL, FROM THE SOUTH.

OUTSIDE OF CHAPEL.

SHRINE OF CHAPEL.

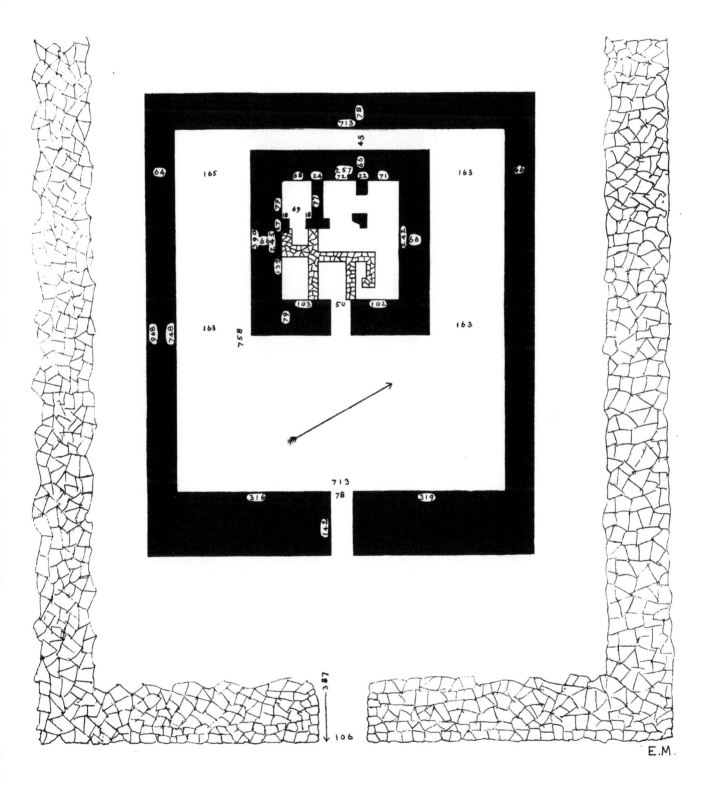

E.M.

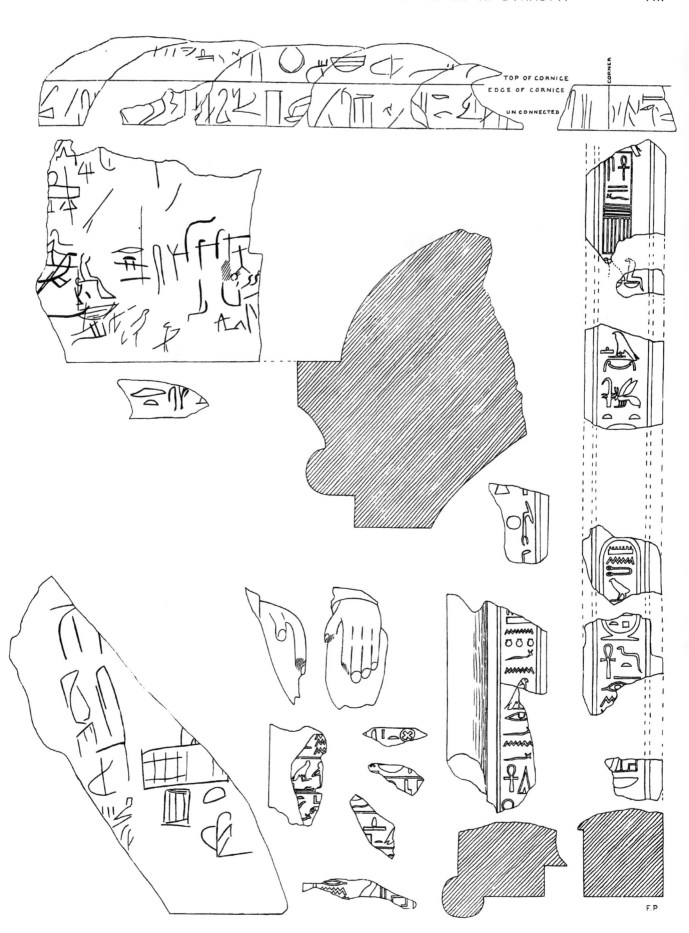

F.P

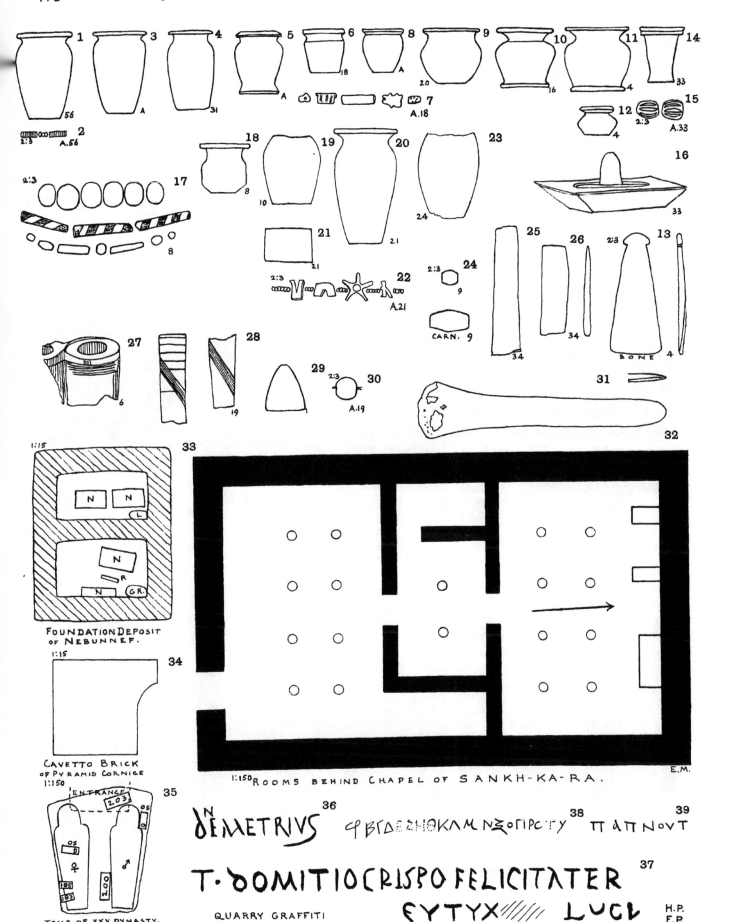

FOUNDATION DEPOSIT
of NEBUNNEF.

CAVETTO BRICK
of PYRAMID CORNICE
1:150

ENTRANCE

TOMB OF XXV DYNASTY.

1:150 ROOMS BEHIND CHAPEL OF SANKH-KA-RA.

E.M.

QUARRY GRAFFITI

ͩEMETRIVS

T·ΔOMITIOCRISPOFELICITATER

ΕΥΤΥΧ///// LVCL

H.P.
F.P.

BLACK TOPPED RED POTTERY.

ALABASTER KOHL VASES.

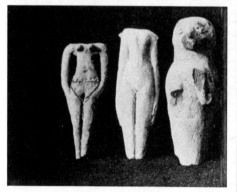

B.19. B.30. B.

BLACK POTTERY BIRD. B.23.

MAULS OF XVIII. DYNASTY.

MAULS OF XII DYNASTY.

B.33

B.45

H.P.

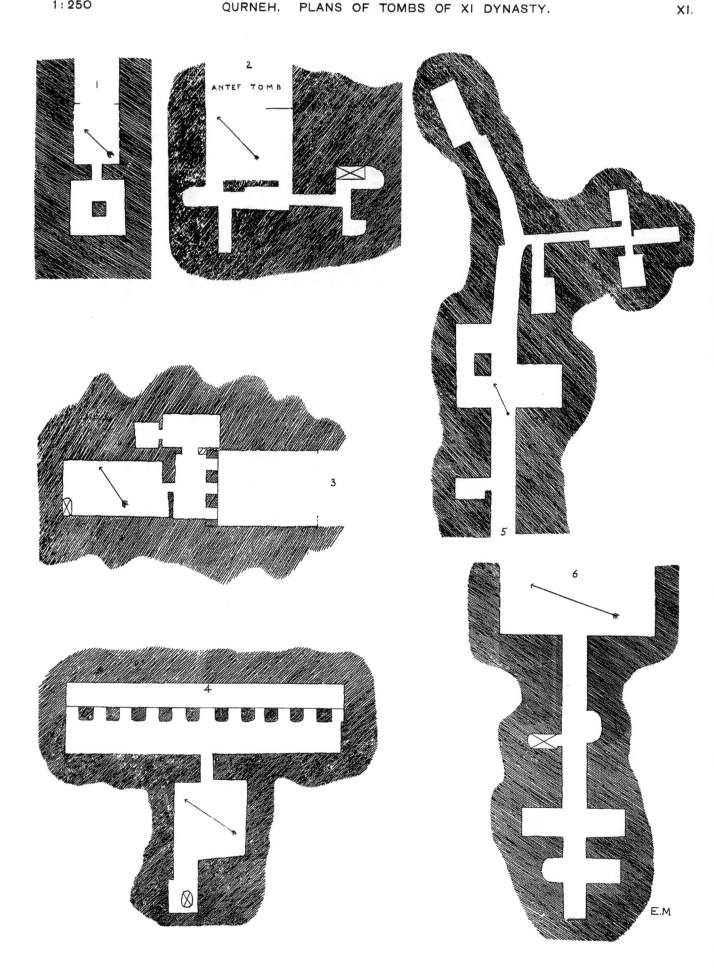

ANTEF TOMB

E.M

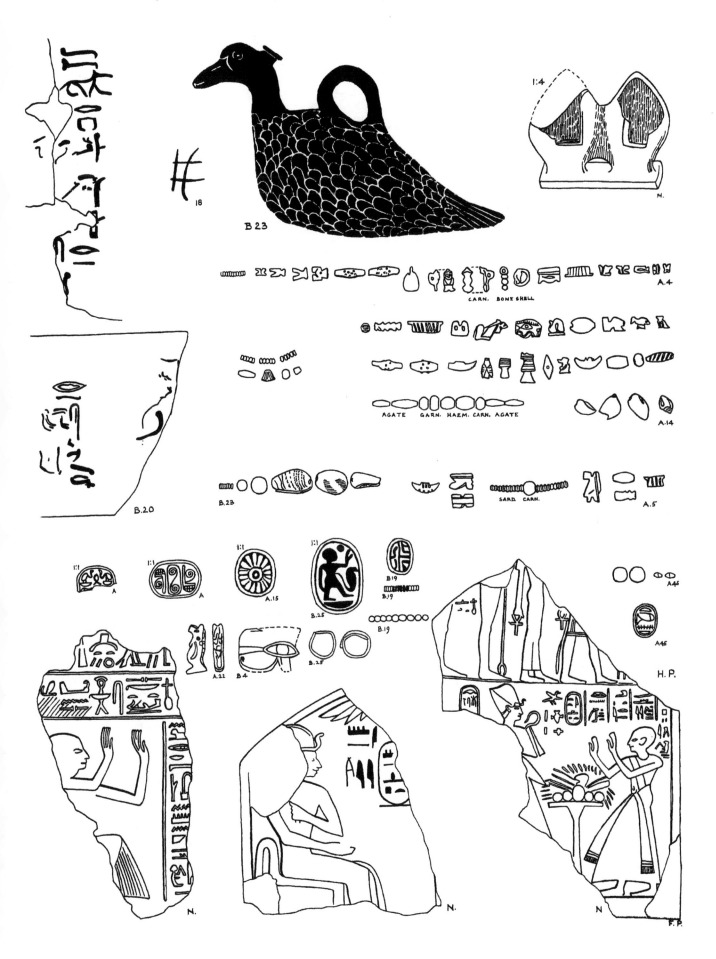

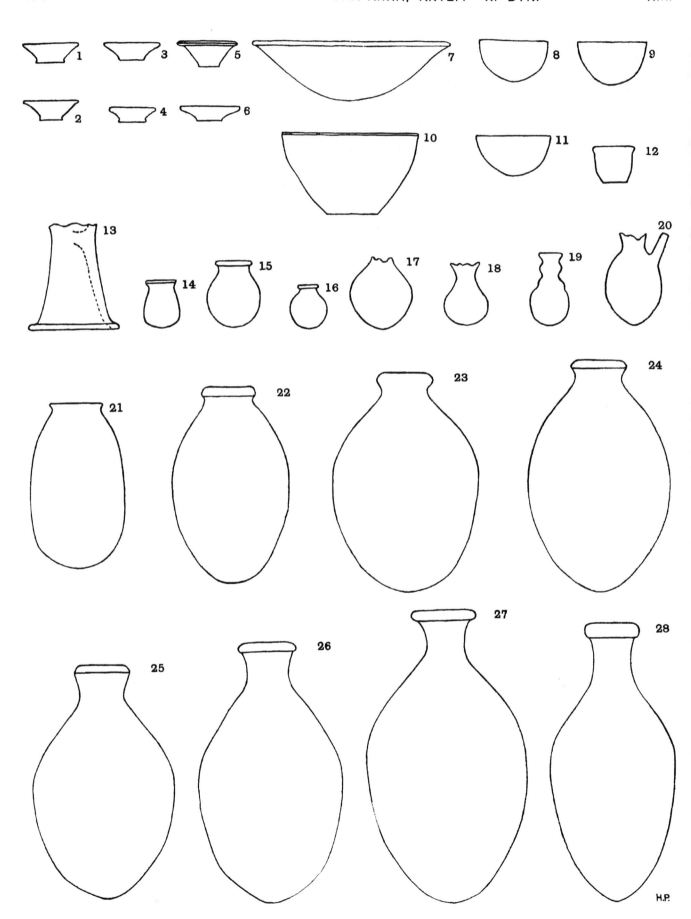

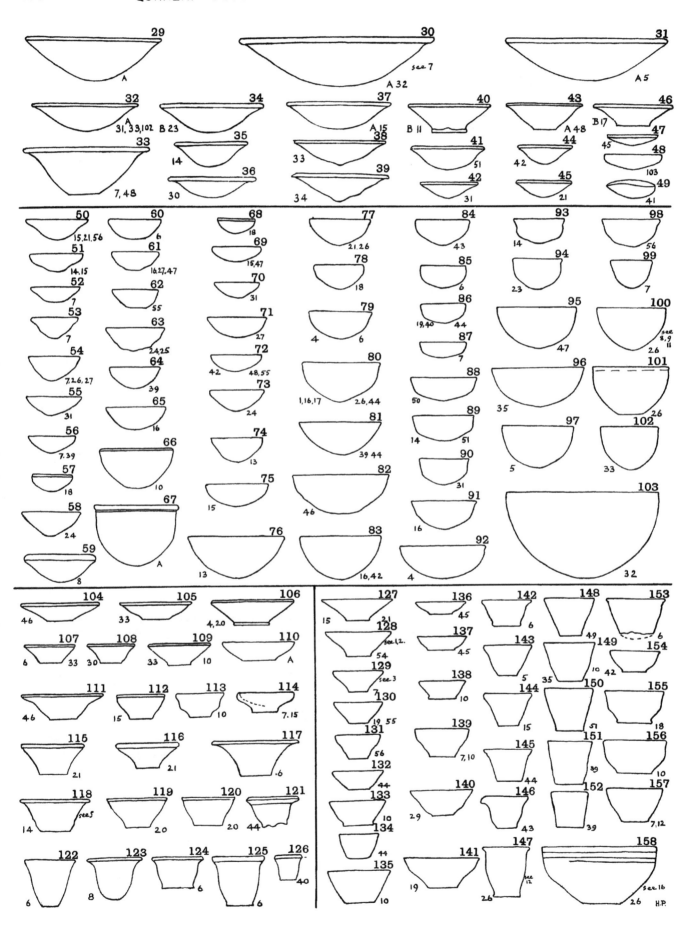

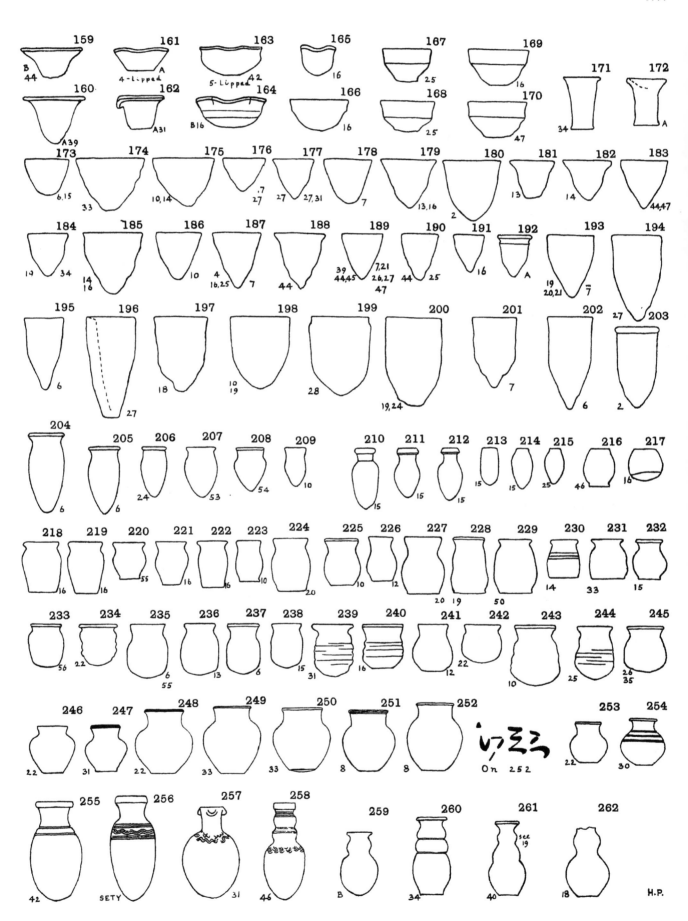

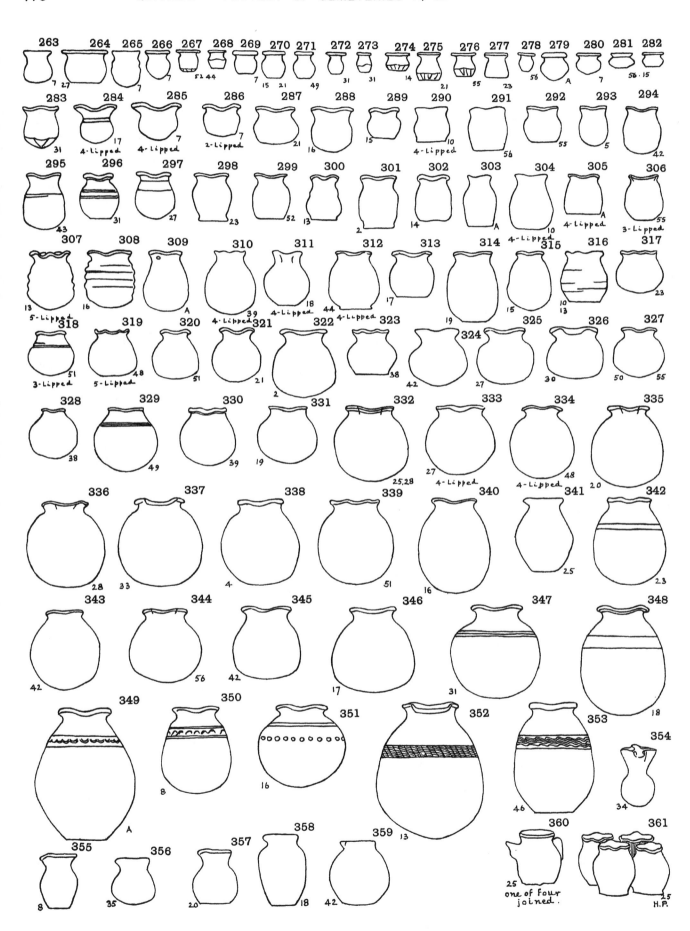

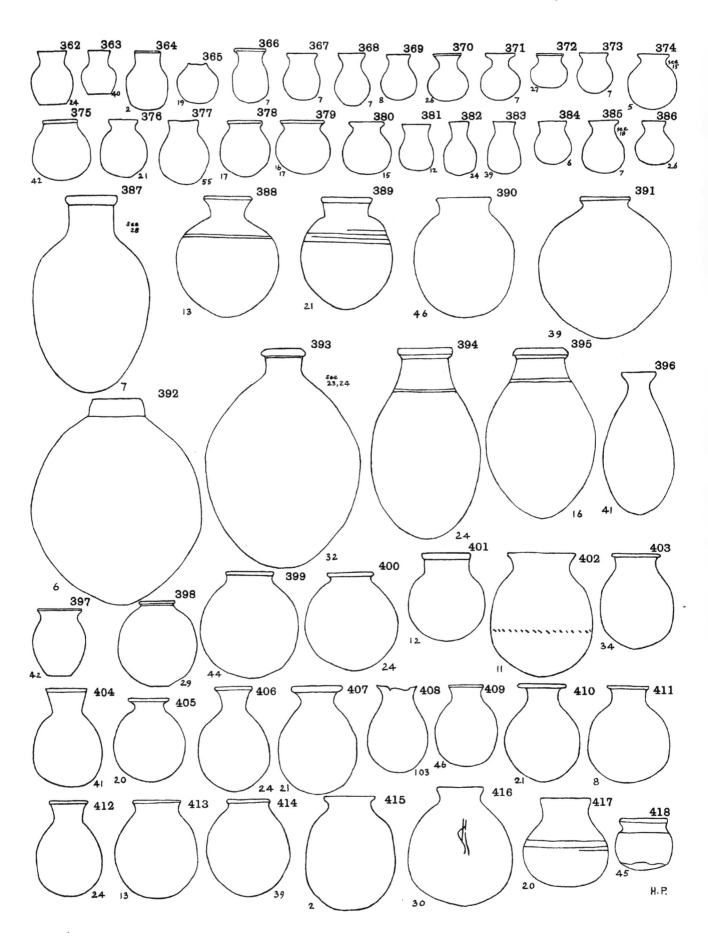

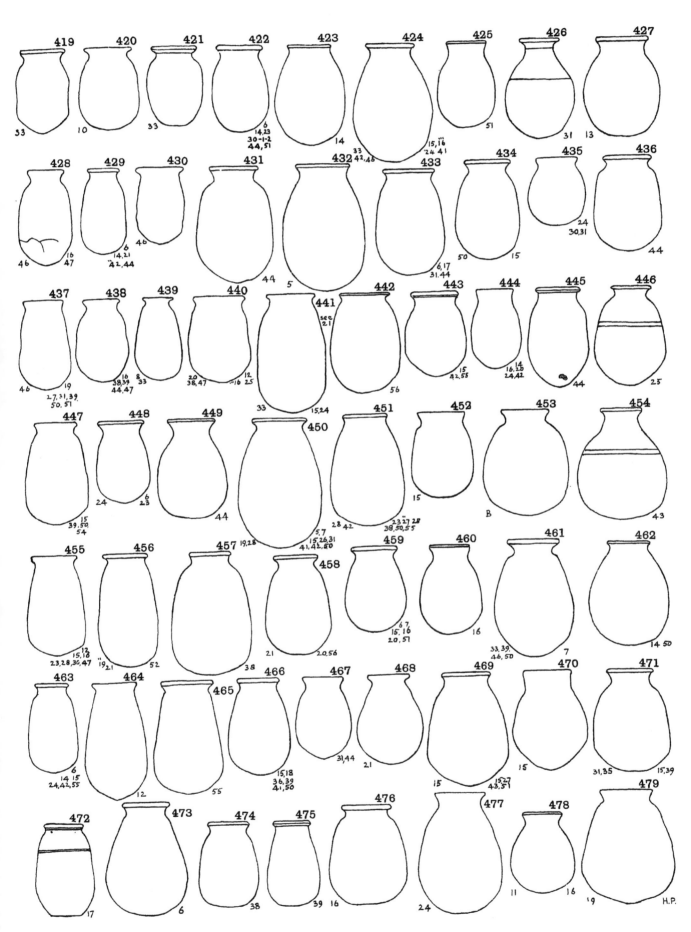

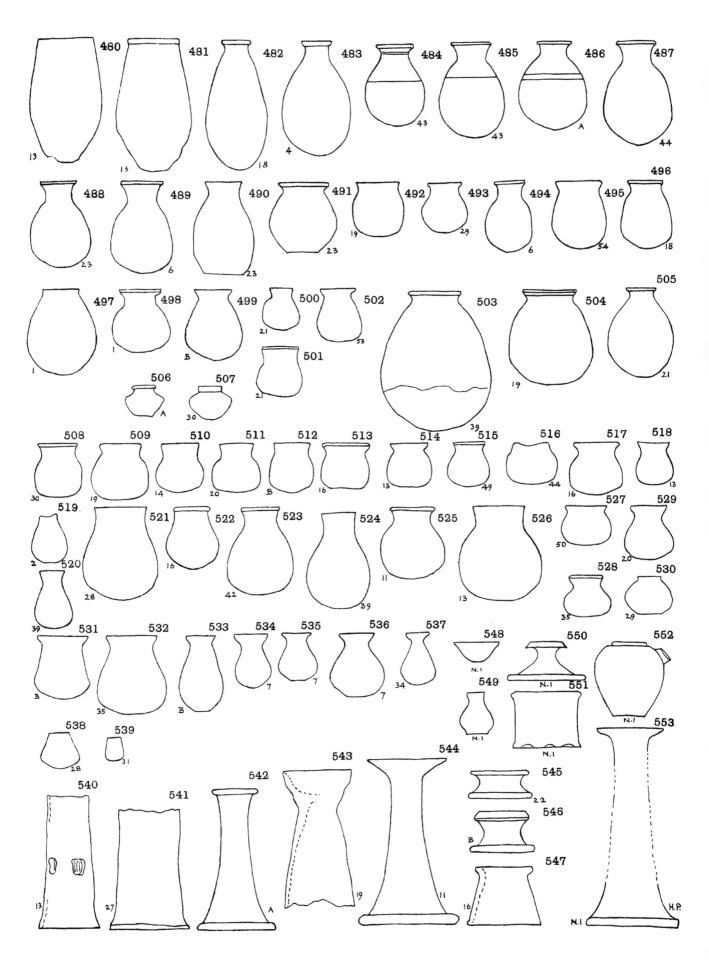

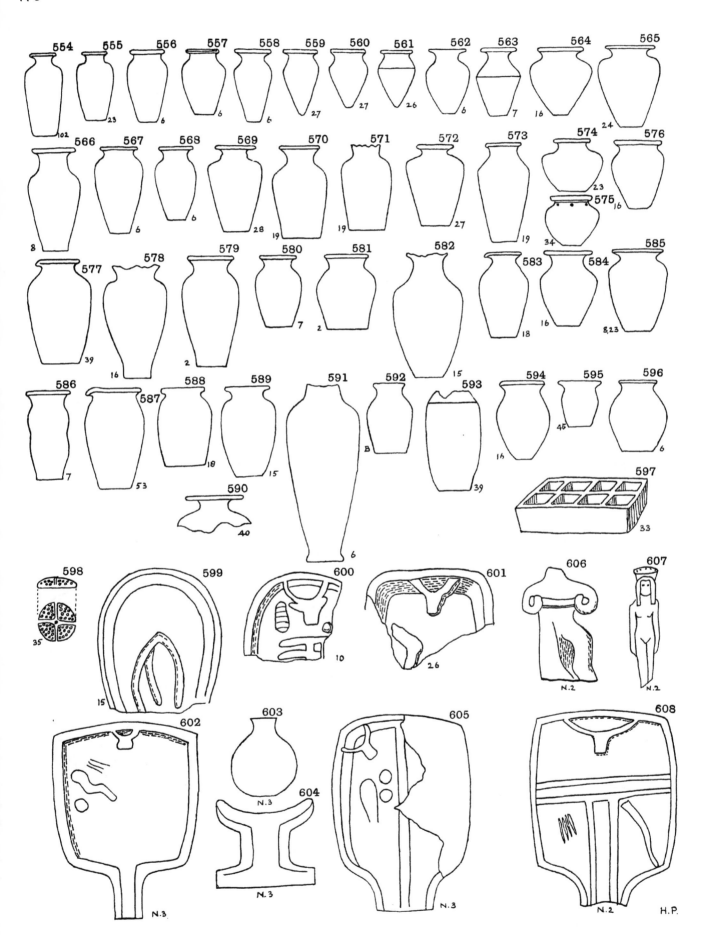

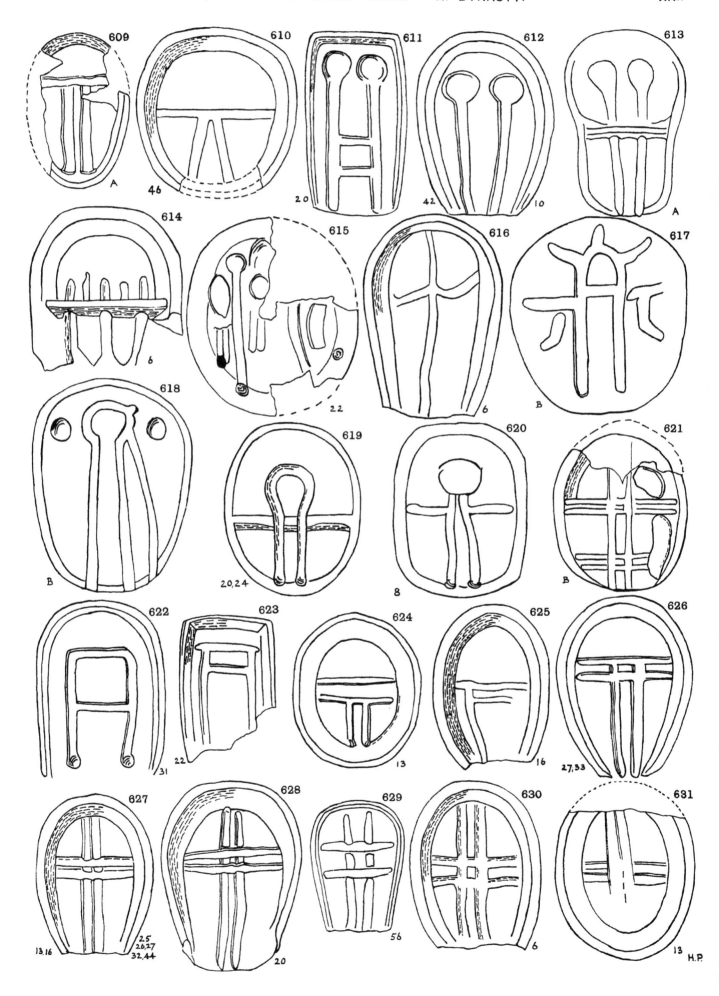

H.P.

POTTERY 1:6

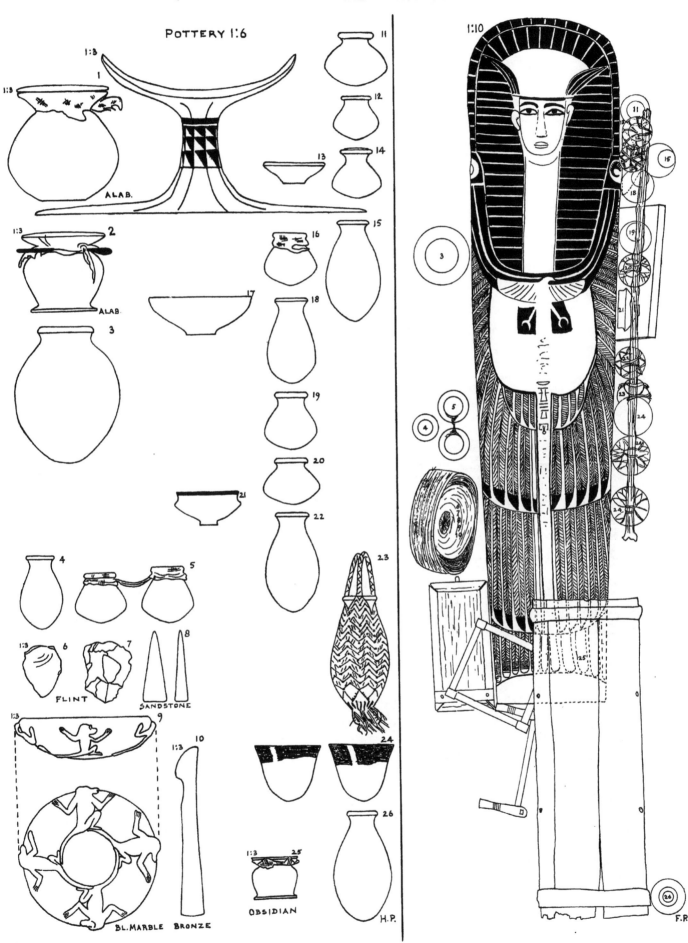

1:3 1

1:3 1

ALAB.

1:3 2

ALAB.

3

4

1:3 6

FLINT

7

8

SANDSTONE

1:3 9

1:3 10

BL. MARBLE BRONZE

11

12

13 14

15

16

17 18

19

20

21 22

23

24

1:3 25

OBSIDIAN

26

H.P.

1:10

3

4 5

F.R

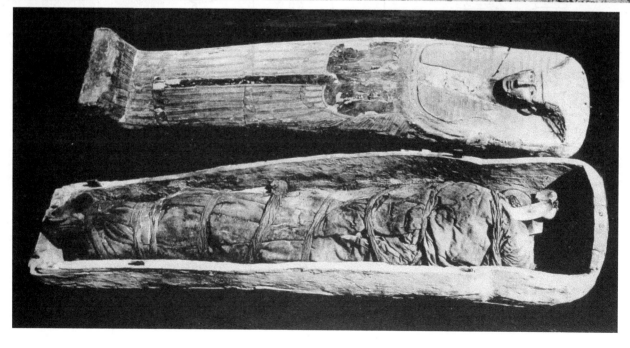

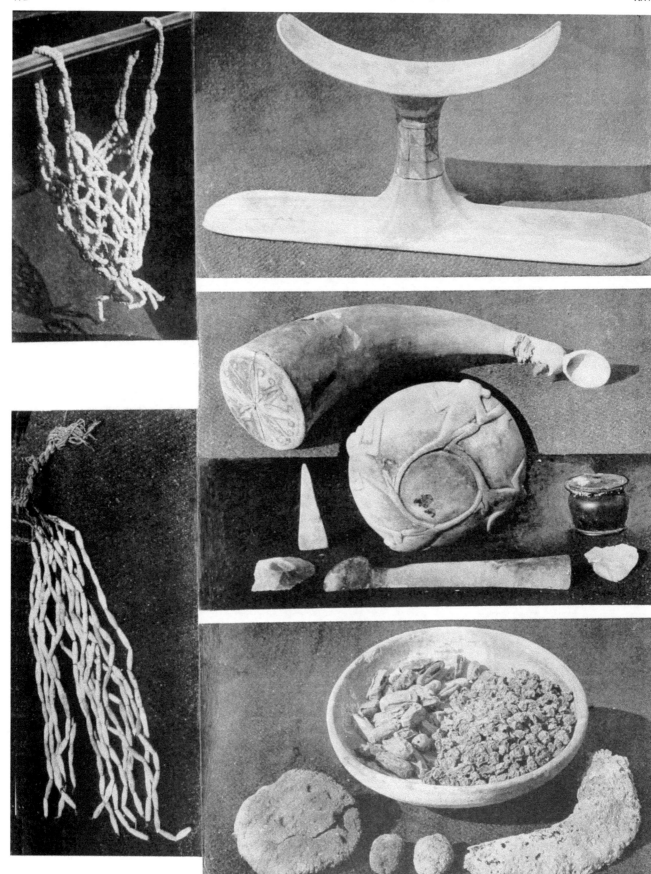

RED POTTERY.

ALABASTER.

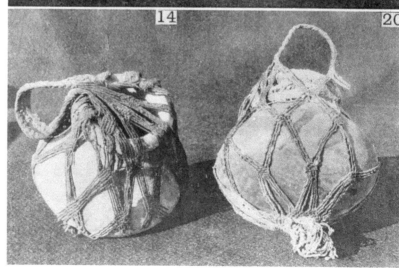

NUMBERS REFER TO PLATE XXII.

3:2

FASTENING OPEN.

3:2

SCARAB.

ELECTRUM BUTTON.

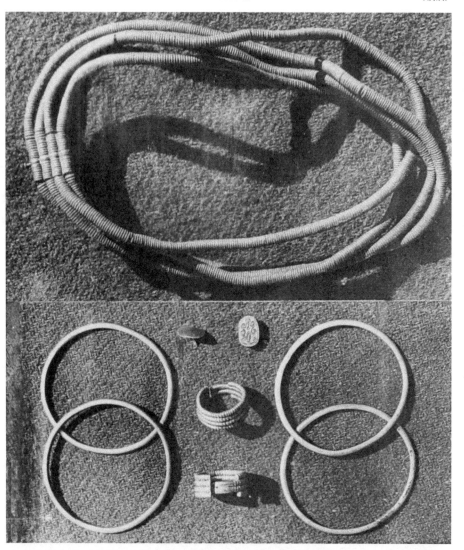

GOLD COLLAR, BANGLES, AND EAR-RINGS.

WEIGHTS.

—o—

		GRAINS.	
Collar	- -	1585.4	20 × 79.3
Bangles	- -	322.7	4 × 80.7
		324.4	4 × 81.1
		325.6	4 × 81.4
		325.8	4 × 81.4
Ear-rings	- -	133.8	
		138.8	
Button	- -	11.7	
Girdle	- -	352	
		3520	

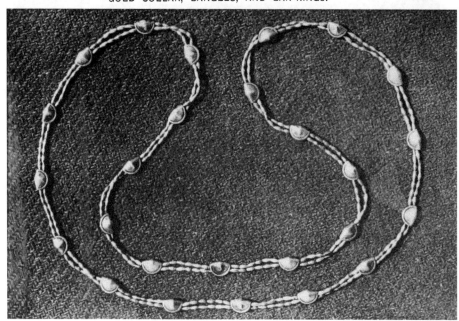

ELECTRUM GIRDLE.

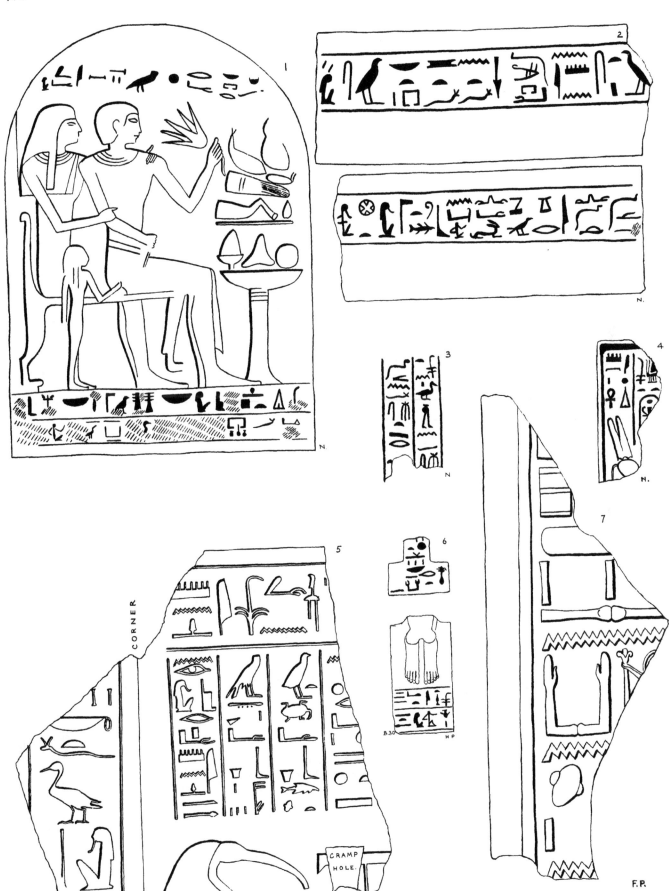

F.P.

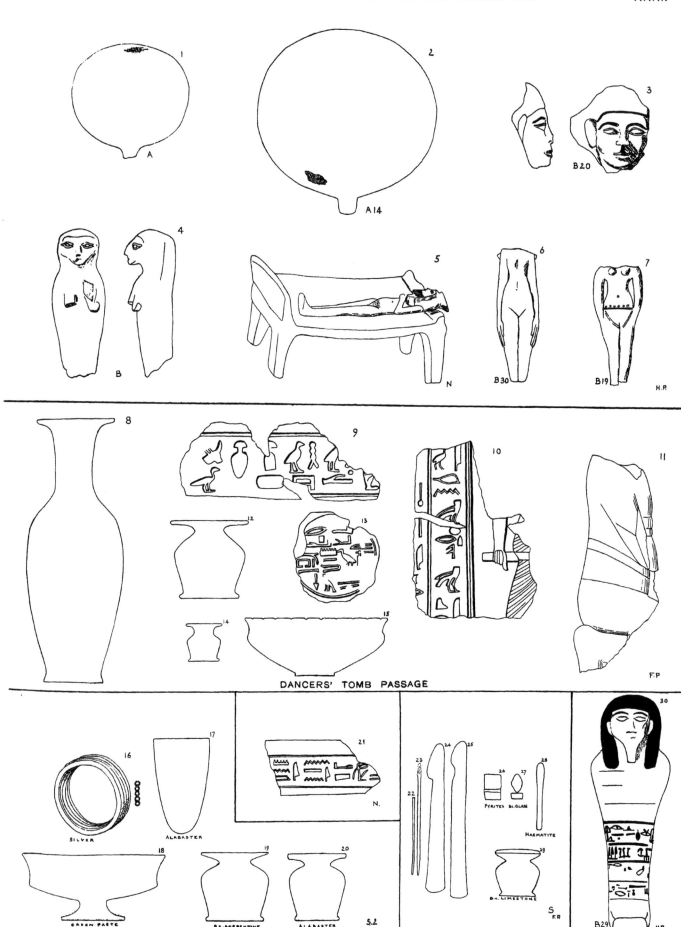

DANCERS' TOMB PASSAGE

LIMESTONE FIGURE.

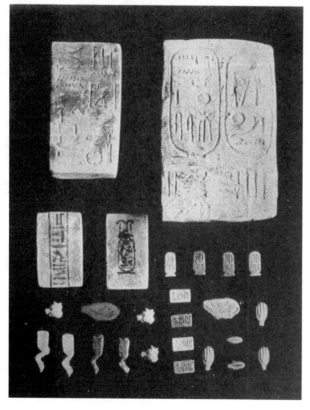

FOUNDATION DEPOSIT OF NEBUNNEF.

TRIAL PIECE.

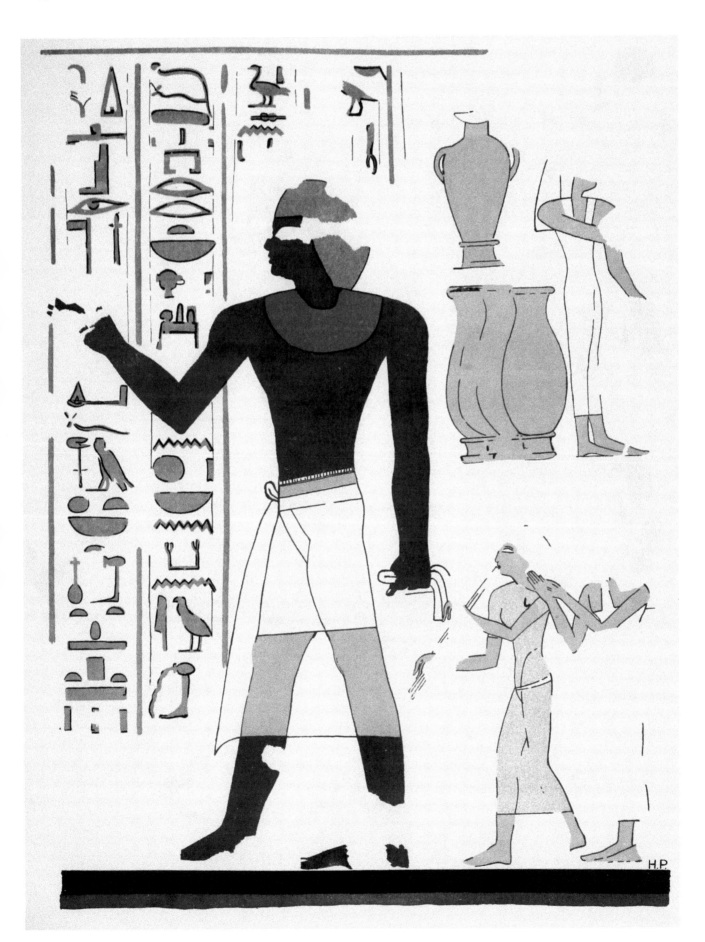

H.P.

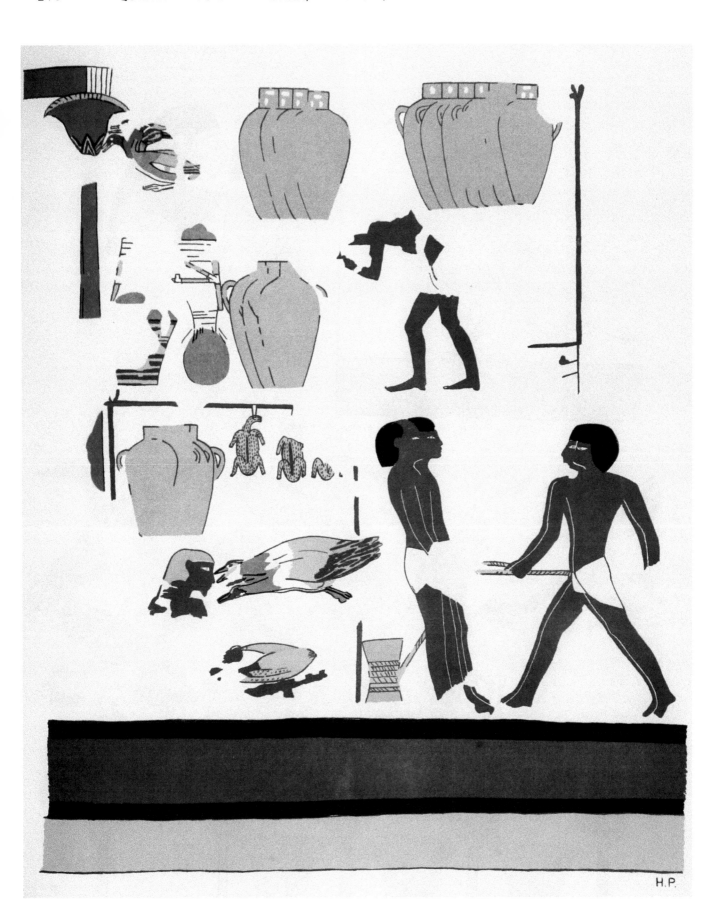

H.P.

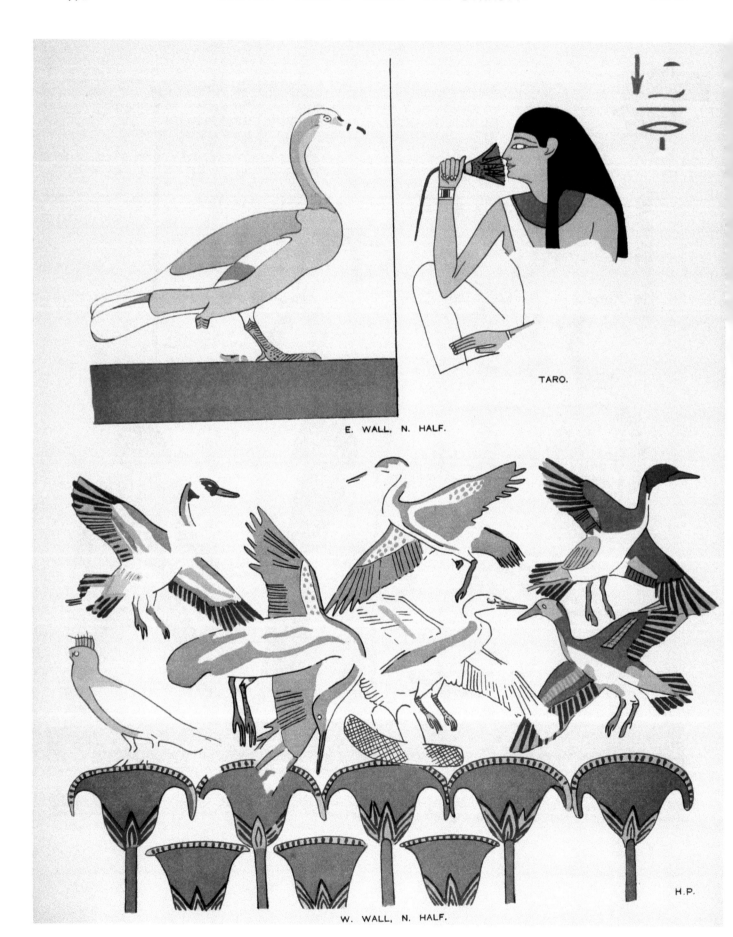

TARO.

E. WALL, N. HALF.

W. WALL, N. HALF.

H.P.

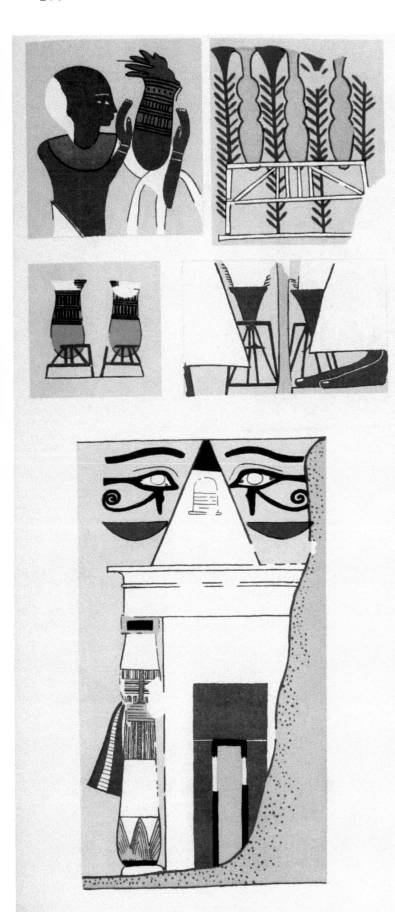

H.P.

H.P.

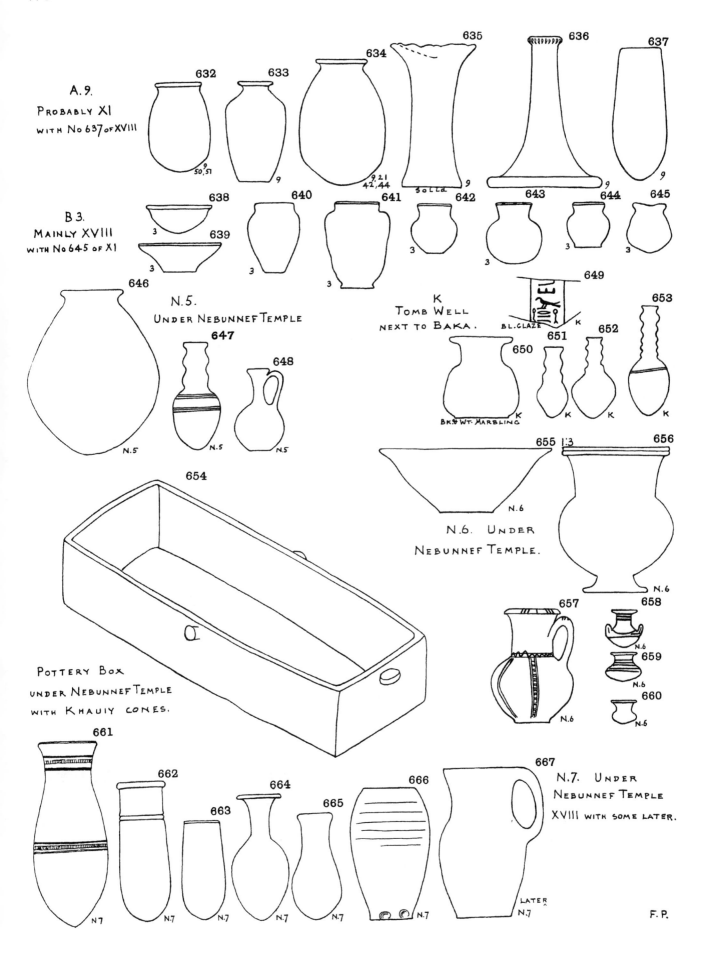

A.9.
PROBABLY XI
WITH No 637 OF XVIII

B 3.
MAINLY XVIII
WITH No 645 OF XI

N.5.
UNDER NEBUNNEF TEMPLE

K
TOMB WELL
NEXT TO BAKA.

N.6. UNDER
NEBUNNEF TEMPLE.

POTTERY BOX
UNDER NEBUNNEF TEMPLE
WITH KHAUIY CONES.

N.7. UNDER
NEBUNNEF TEMPLE
XVIII WITH SOME LATER.

F.P.

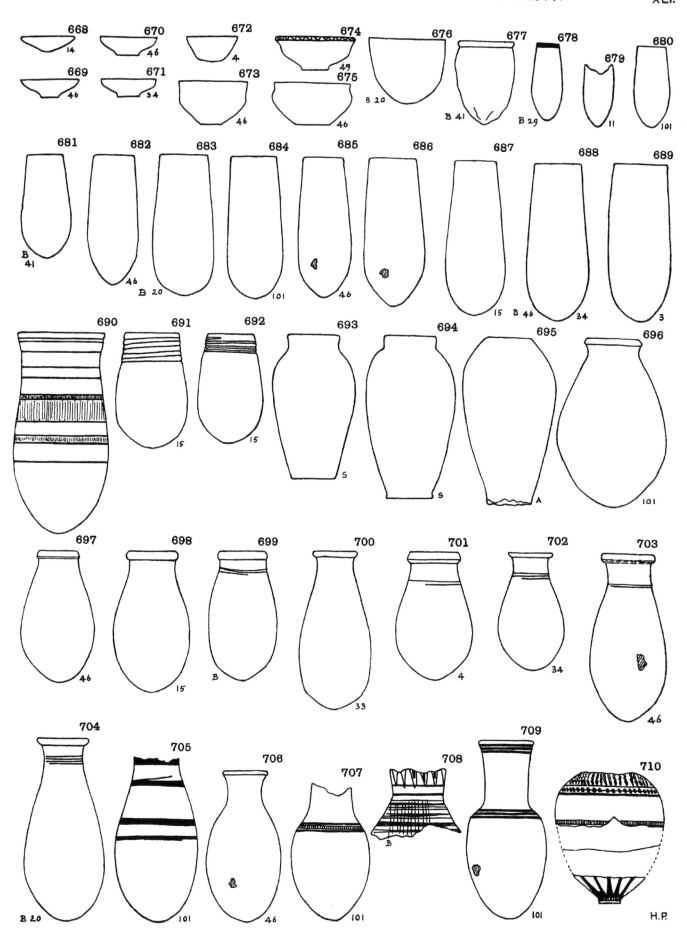

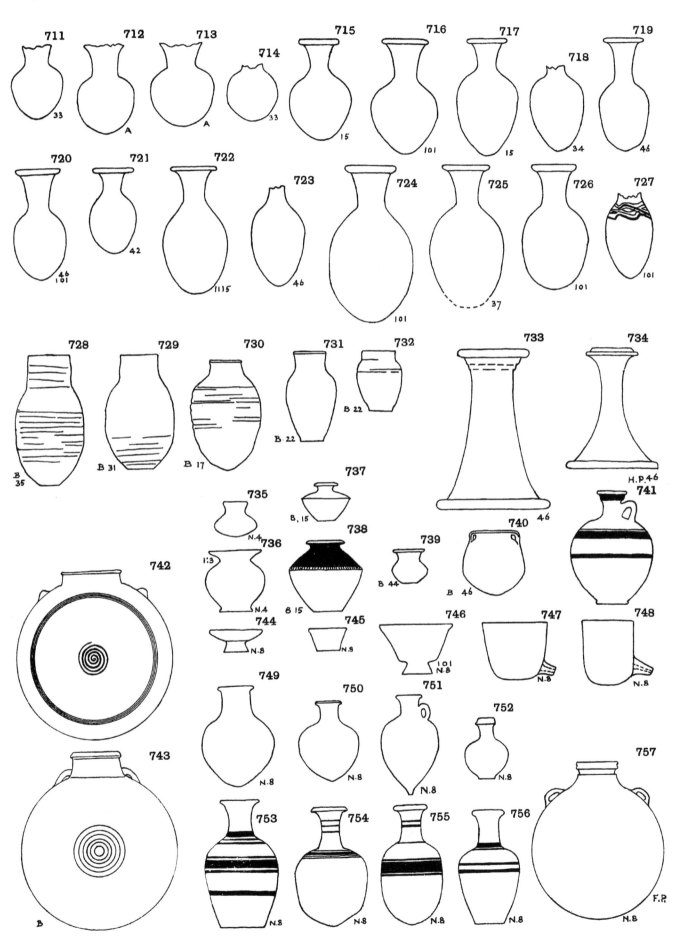

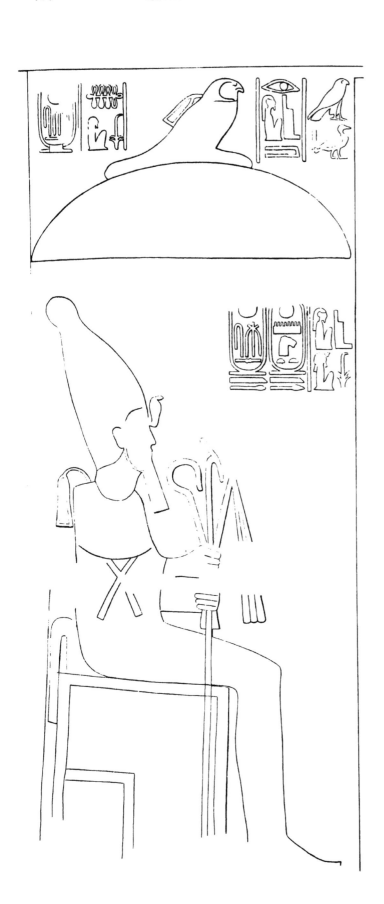

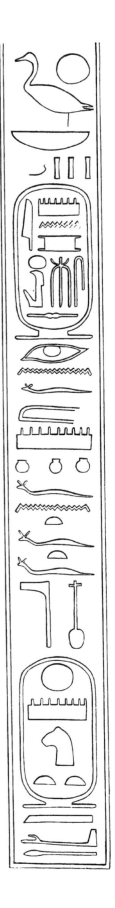

H.P.

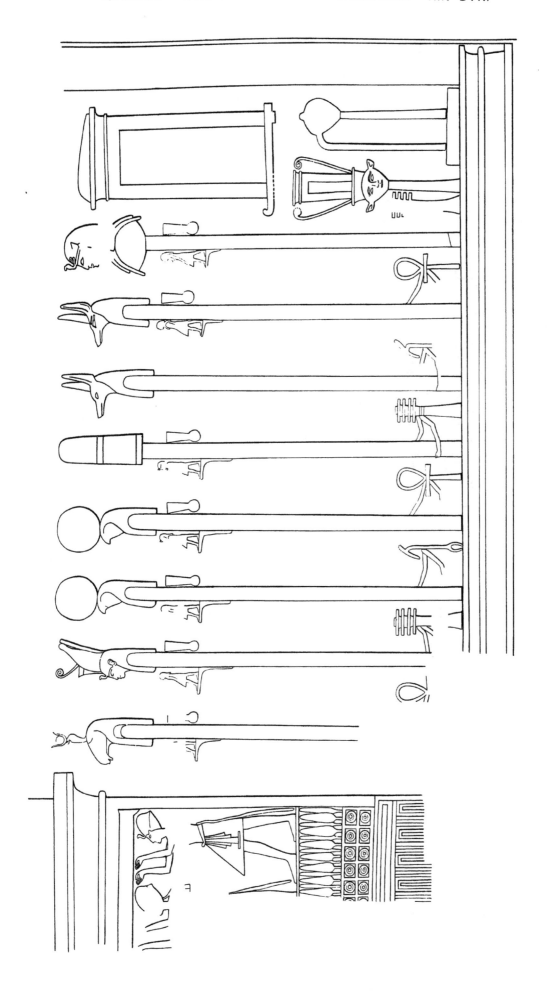

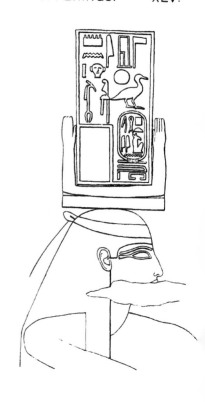

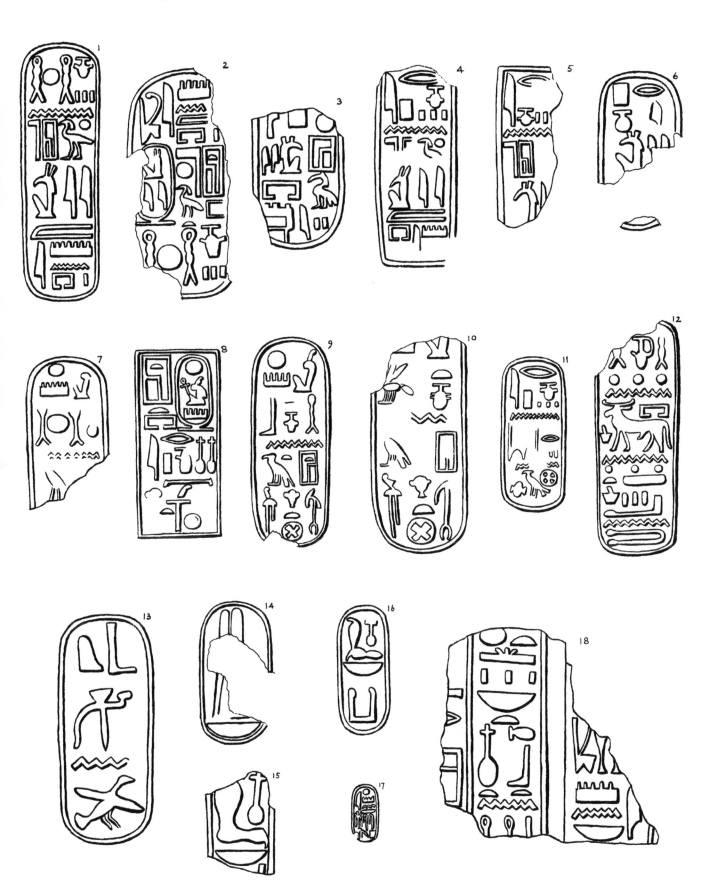

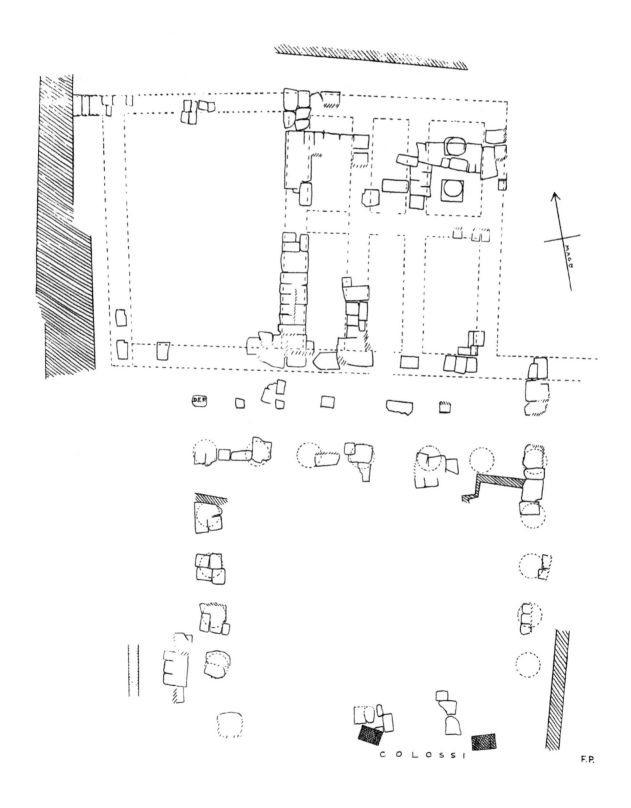

COLOSSI

F.P.

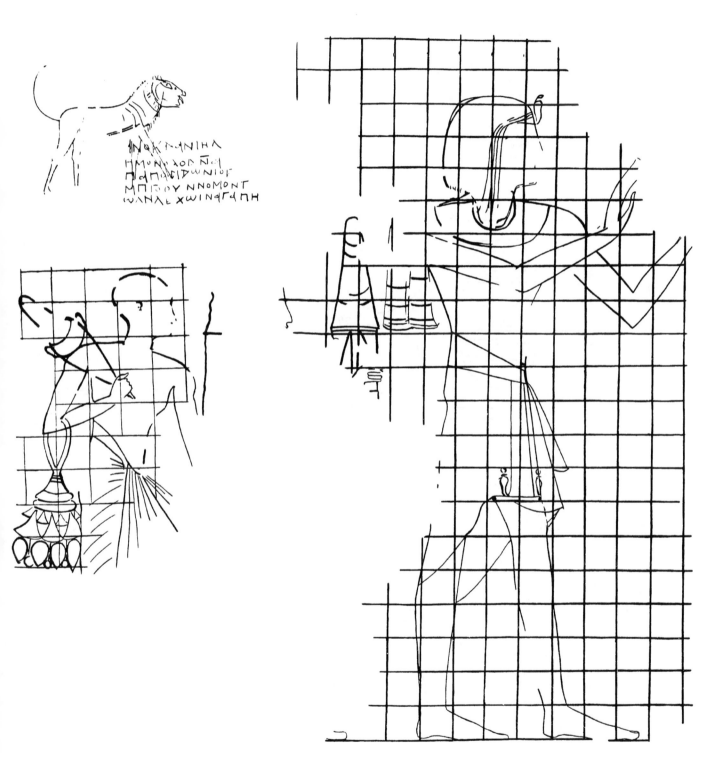

H.P.

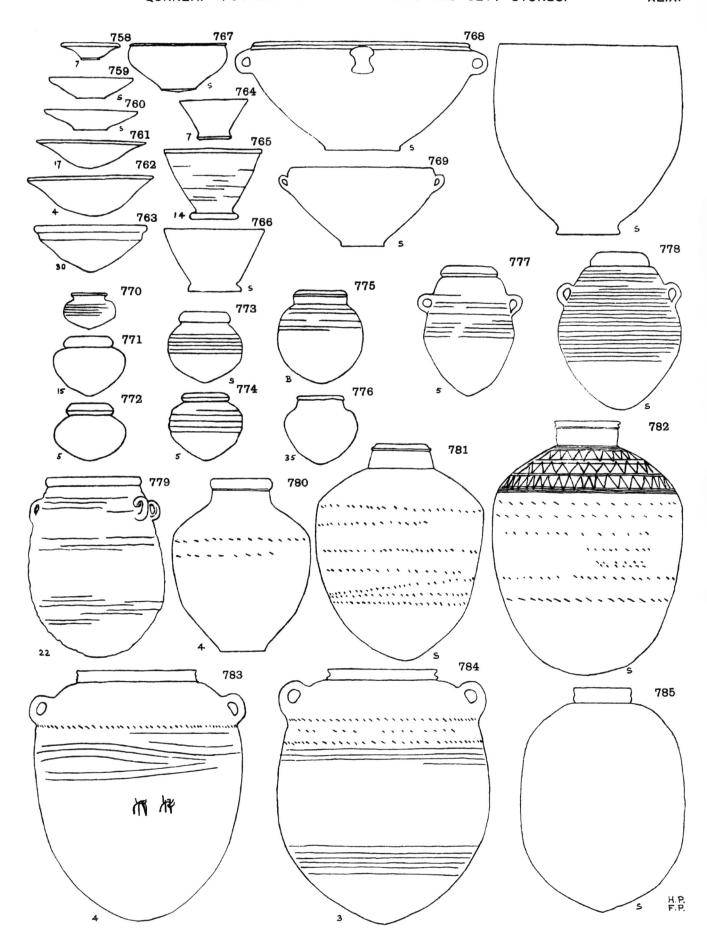

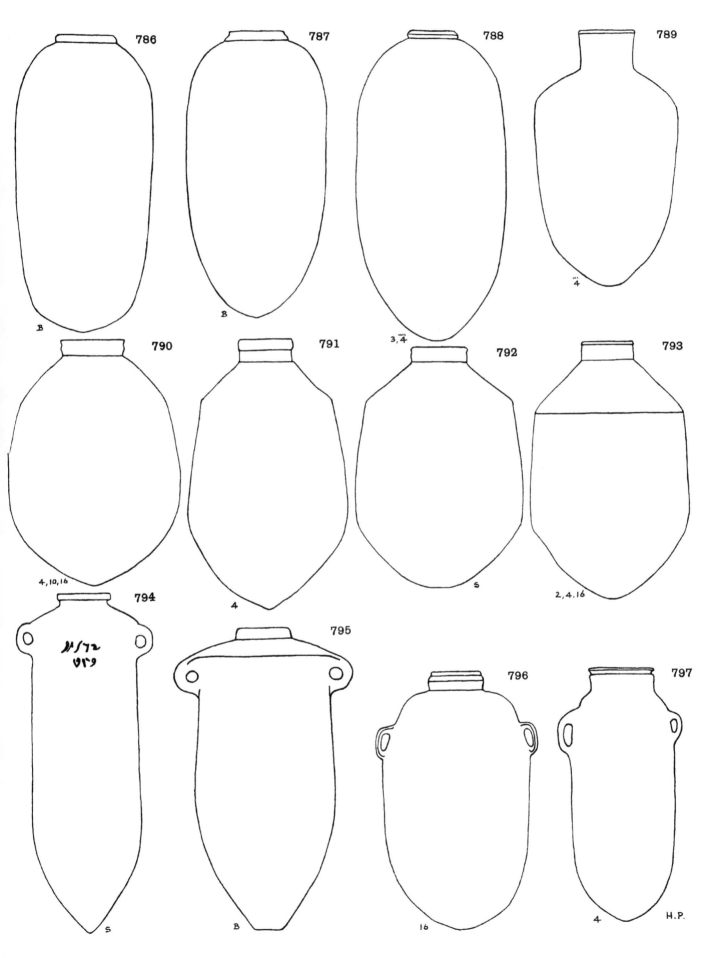

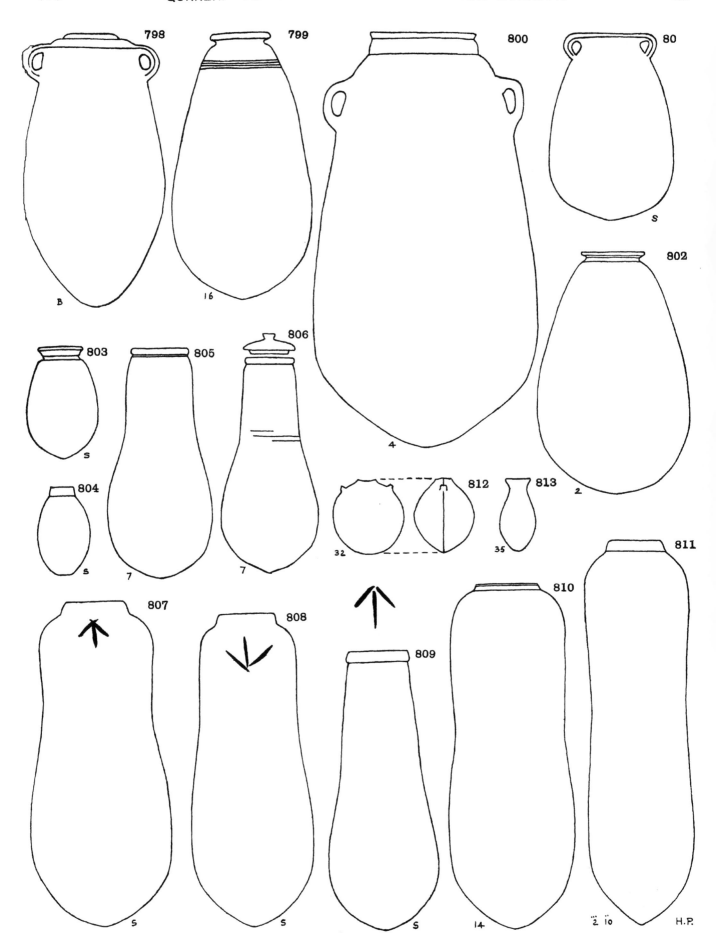

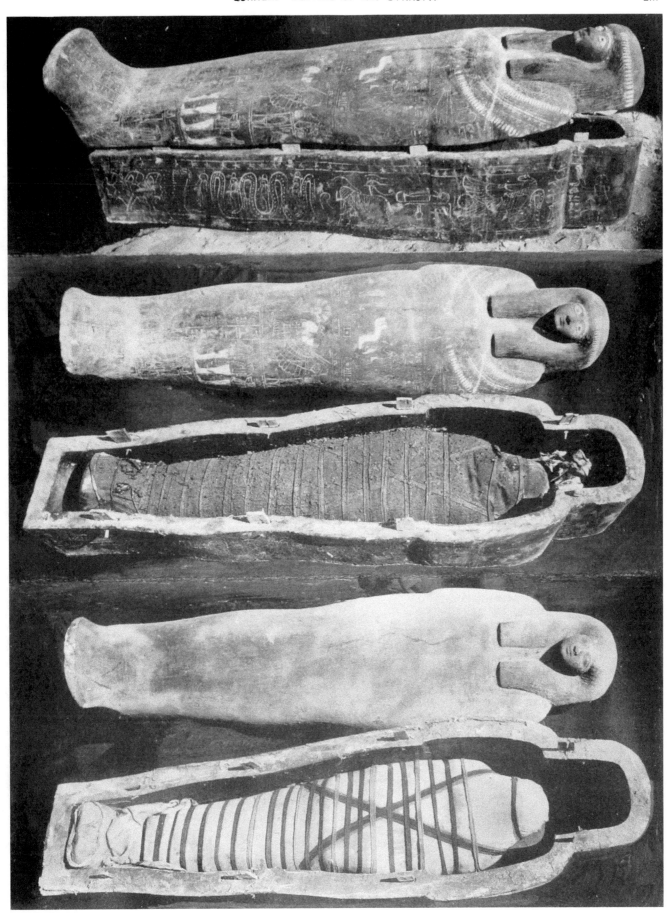

LOTUS FROM BURIAL.

OSIRIS FIGURES, USHABTI BOXES, AND USHABTIS.

ROMAN GUARD HOUSE,
COPTIC HERMITAGE AND PILLAR
DWELLING.

PILLAR DWELLING FROM ABOVE.

MODERN SOUL HOUSES BY SHEYKH'S TOMB.

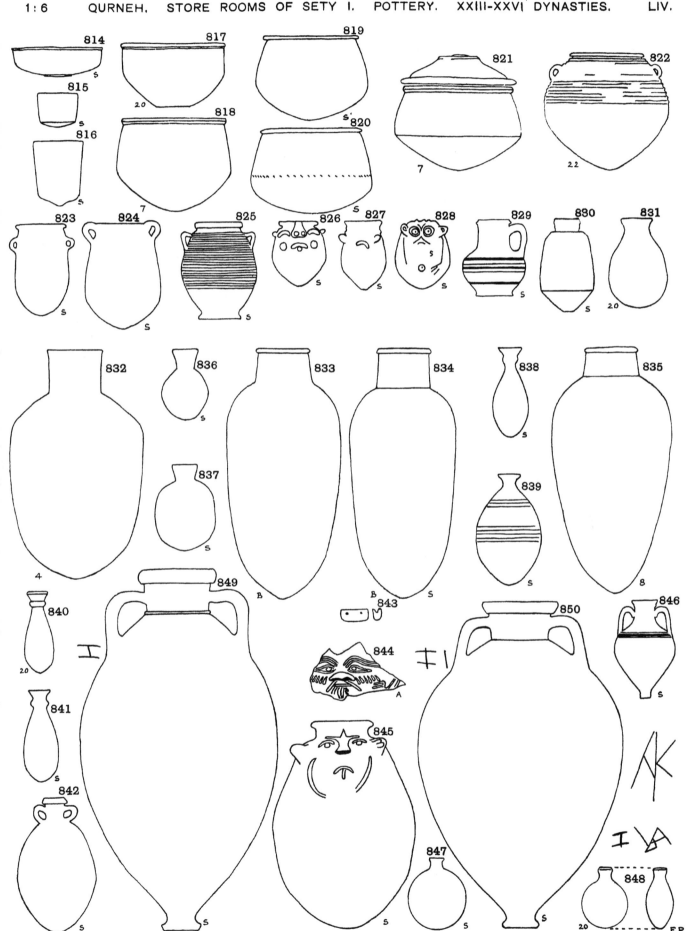

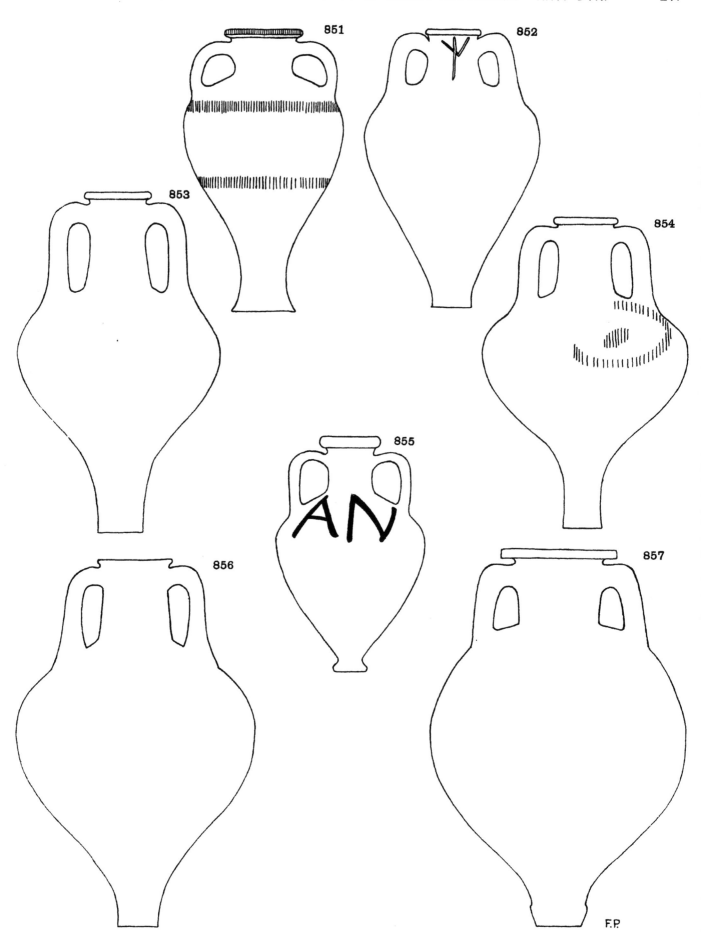

F.P.

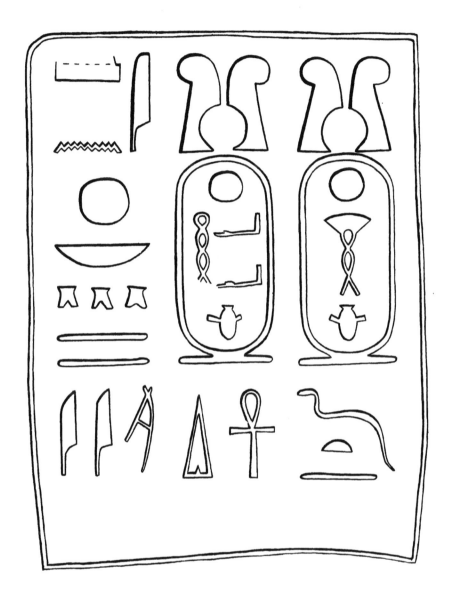

H.P.

For EU product safety concerns, contact us at Calle de José Abascal, 56–1°,
28003 Madrid, Spain or eugpsr@cambridge.org.

www.ingramcontent.com/pod-product-compliance
Ingram Content Group UK Ltd.
Pitfield, Milton Keynes, MK11 3LW, UK
UKHW051029150625
459647UK00023B/2860